The Responsible Globalist

HASSAN DAMLUJI

The Responsible Globalist

*What Citizens of the World Can Learn
from Nationalism*

ALLEN LANE
an imprint of
PENGUIN BOOKS

ALLEN LANE

UK | USA | Canada | Ireland | Australia
India | New Zealand | South Africa

Allen Lane is part of the Penguin Random House group of companies
whose addresses can be found at global.penguinrandomhouse.com

First published 2019
001

Copyright © Hassan Damluji, 2019

The moral right of the author has been asserted

Set in 9.75/13 pt Sabon LT Std
Typeset by Jouve (UK), Milton Keynes
Printed and bound in Great Britain by Clays Ltd, Elcograf S.p.A.

A CIP catalogue record for this book is available from the British Library

ISBN: 978-0-241-35509-1

www.greenpenguin.co.uk

MIX
Paper from
responsible sources
FSC® C018179

Penguin Random House is committed to a
sustainable future for our business, our readers
and our planet. This book is made from Forest
Stewardship Council® certified paper.

*For Anna and Rafi – the tribe within which
I most profoundly belong.*

The entire earth is my homeland and all its people my fellow citizens.

Gibran Khalil Gibran[1]

Contents

Introduction 1

Globalists and Nationalists 9

Principle 1: Leave no one out 30

Principle 2: Define the mission, and the enemy 47

Principle 3: Defend the nation-state 67

Principle 4: If you love mobility, let it go 81

Principle 5: The winners must pay to play 100

Principle 6: The 'rules-based system'
needs better rules 122

Conclusion: A Choice of Paths 143

Acknowledgements 153

Notes 155

Index 177

Introduction

A nation is born when a few people decide that it should be.
Paul Ignotus[1]

We know that we need to cooperate in order to solve our biggest problems, from climate change to poverty, disease and war. We are horrified that in so many countries politics is turning inwards, because we know that this will leave our most pressing challenges unaddressed. But globalists – people who want more international cooperation and stronger global institutions – are yet to present a compelling vision. Too often we seem like defenders of the status quo. Too often we think that it is sufficient to tinker with the rules of the global economy or harangue political leaders who turn their back on international agreements.

In this book I argue that if we want the global system to work better we need to learn something from nationalism. Identity matters. Group solidarity matters. Successful institutions can only sit on top of societies based on trust and a belief in common belonging.

So if you want global institutions, you need people everywhere to feel a strong globalist identity. That does not mean erasing or even diminishing other forms of belonging. I am deeply committed to my British identity, but also proud of being a Londoner, a supporter of Brentford Football Club and a member of my immediate family, not to mention my ties to my parents' countries of origin: Ireland and Iraq. Every reader will have various groups to which they simultaneously belong. All of these complex identities can continue to thrive as we build on top of them a stronger feeling of common humanity.[2]

What kind of common bond can support the level of global co-operation we need? There is only one form of human identity that has been able to tie millions – even billions – of people of every different religion and political persuasion into a single rules-based system. That is the idea of the nation. Born at the dawn of the Industrial Revolution as a byproduct of modernity, 'the nation' has been a remarkably successful idea.[3] It has convinced strangers who have never met that they should trust each other and cooperate without requiring of them any belief other than that they belong to the group.

This concept has enabled some of our greatest achievements: democracy, the welfare state, unprecedented public safety, and many more. None of these would be possible without the basic trust between citizens that the myth of common nationhood brought. But it has fallen down because nations have been conceived in a way that excludes most people. That has led to internally coherent, trust-based societies that are nevertheless prepared to inflict unspeakable cruelty on people who fall beyond the circle of trust. Sometimes these 'others' have been foreigners to be vanquished in battle; often they have been people living inside the borders of the state who are felt not to belong and must therefore be removed or exterminated. And despite the benefits they have provided for their members, the limited national identities we have created do not allow for global problem-solving. Two hundred totally separate nation-states might all provide basic health care to their citizens but would have very little to offer against problems that cross borders, like Ebola or climate change. In a globalized economy, they would have insufficient power to prevent catastrophic crashes and soaring inequality.

Supporters of open politics therefore often call for an end to nationalism. They see a cosmopolitan future where we all respect each other's differences and learn to accept diversity.[4] This is a noble aim, but on its own it is insufficient. We can never escape our instinctive tribalism.[5] Like our other destructive instincts, it must be channelled in a positive direction, rather than ignored. Many of the world's most dangerous political forces today are the result of elites trying to brush strongly held group identities under the carpet. What nationalists understand all too well is that for people to cooperate effectively they need not only to respect each other's differences but also to believe that they have something very important in common.

What if we were to build a truly global nation? What if we could create a narrative of common belonging that all humans bought into, establishing the kind of trust and reciprocal obligations across humanity that members of a national community currently feel? Most of us already have a strong sense that humans share something important in common and that we all deserve some minimal level of respect from each other. Gone are the days of state-sponsored slavery on an industrial scale. But human solidarity remains weak when compared to the bonds that tie together a national community. People who willingly part with a huge proportion of their income in taxes, to be spent on fellow citizens whom they have never met, are often furious that just 1 or 2 per cent is sent abroad to help the world's very poorest people.[6] West Germans were prepared to spend €2 trillion on supporting their co-nationals in East Germany during the unification process in the 1990s.[7] But when Greece was struggling under the weight of its debts in the following decade, even the plight of this fellow EU state did not move Germans to open their country's coffers.[8]

A global national sentiment would lead to very different politics. It would no longer be viable, when faced with the international spill-overs caused by refugee crises, economic disasters or disease, to bury our heads in the sand and pretend it does not affect us. Answering the challenges to globalization through protectionism and reduced cooperation would seem as ludicrous as Londoners responding to poverty in the North of England by building a wall around the capital. A global nation would provide the moral and social framework to support the basic truth that, as humans, we do have a common ancestry, we are mutually dependent and we are bound by a common destiny on this shrinking planet. Without that moral and social framework, the self-defeating law of the jungle in international politics will continue and the people and institutions that seek to solve global problems will never be fully funded or empowered.

In this book I make three related claims. The first is that a global nation is possible. The conditions are now in place for the myth of nationhood to be stretched beyond even the giant states of India and China (each of which already contains as many people as the entire planet did 150 years ago),[9] to encompass all 7 billion humans alive today. The second claim is that anti-globalist sentiment is driven by the injustices that define our global community. People are not congenitally anti-globalist but, when presented with a system in which they seem set to lose out, they are inclined to reject global cooperation altogether. The third claim, on which the bulk of this book is focused, is that we can and should formulate a more appealing, inclusive globalist credo. In doing so, we will stand a far better chance of building human solidarity around the idea of a united, global nation.

Now may seem a particularly strange time to argue that a global nation is possible. In the age of Brexit and Donald Trump, the conventional wisdom is that 'globalists' stand on the wrong side of history. Many of the people I interviewed for this book struck a pessimistic tone. Current and former senior officials at the Obama and the Chan Zuckerberg foundations told me that there were too many crises, and too much work to do, at home in America to even think about the idea of global unity. Sir Nick Clegg, former UK Deputy Prime Minister and now Facebook's Vice-president for Global Affairs and Communications, told me that his high hopes in the 1980s of a progressively more cooperative world had gradually receded in the face of the experience of the continued power of nationalism. Yanis Varoufakis, former Greek Finance Minister and cofounder of a new pan-European movement, DiEM25, told me that he agreed with what he called 'universal citizenship' but that the word 'global' is now so toxic I should find a synonym instead. To set out a case in defence of globalism at this point in time, he said, would be 'like a left-wing party trying to win an election in Europe by campaigning under the banner of Communism'.

I do not dispute that we live in concerning times for advocates of a cosmopolitan, collaborative world. But I do want to moderate the anxiety so that it can be turned into positive energy. We need to step outside the prism of North Atlantic bias that afflicts many discussions of 'world events'. This will tell us that the ethno-nationalist rejection of global cooperation is not on the ascendancy everywhere. Global solidarity is still rising in the world's most populous and fastest-growing economies. As I will show in the next chapter, a majority of people around the world say they view themselves 'more as a citizen of the world than of any country', and the proportion is highest in countries like India, China and the Philippines. A majority of people in every country surveyed, including those racked by populist anger, believe that 'for issues like the environment, international bodies should have enforcement powers'.[10] These are surprising results for a world that has supposedly rejected globalism.

The reason that globalist identity is still becoming stronger is that the processes which originally propelled nationalist feeling within smaller geographical limits – universal education, linguistic convergence, mass media, improved mobility – are now operating globally. As long as these processes remain in place, the stage will be set for a global national identity to emerge. That may be hard to imagine today, but similar startling changes have happened in the past. In 1783 Johann Kaspar Riesbeck wrote that: '[Germans'] pride and feelings for the fatherland relate solely to that part of Germany where they were born. The rest of their countrymen are as much strangers to them as are all foreigners.'[11] Within a hundred years, German unification was complete. Today, it is almost impossible to imagine Germans being divided into more than 400 different states, as they were in Riesbeck's day. This mindset change took time, but it was not merely the result of blind historical processes. Where nations have formed, it is because the idea of a common identity has been actively championed and has captured the imagination of the masses.

The idea that we are all 'citizens of the world' is a powerful one, but many people remain unconvinced. That is understandable. The latest wave of economic globalization since 1980 has created unprecedented wealth, lifting billions out of poverty and producing a new global middle class while making the very richest people even richer. But for lower-skilled people in rich countries, as well as the world's very poorest people, there has been no improvement in their economic position for forty years. In relative terms, they have gone backwards. Many have even seen absolute declines in their incomes.

On top of this, many communities see a threat to their identity. The promulgation of global mainstream culture, both in the mass media and through the decisions of an increasingly globalized political elite, can feel like an attempt to eliminate their traditional way of life. In rich countries, mass immigration seems to be changing communities beyond recognition, with voters feeling powerless to control the pace of change.

Finally, many see the world system as intensely unjust. Presided over by a gang of five nuclear-powered permanent members of the UN Security Council, of whom four are majority-white and majority-Christian countries, the global political system can look like a parody of the human-rights rhetoric its leaders so often espouse. Even in the most powerful countries, many people feel that the global system has been hijacked by unanswerable elites with no faith in democracy.

Two of the most visible manifestations of the anger that these forces have produced are the ethno-nationalist movements of Europe and North America – from 'Trumpublicans', to Alternative für Deutschland (AfD) through to Viktor Orbán's Fidesz party; and the spectrum of political Islam – ranging from the merely angry (Erdoğan in Turkey, the Muslim Brotherhood in Egypt) to the brutally violent (Islamic State and Al-Qaeda). All of these very different movements are united by a desire to unwind elements of the global system that seem to be undermining the incomes, identities and fair treatment of their constituents. In doing so, they are all engaged in a quixotic quest to restore an imagined golden age from an often poorly understood past.

Globalists tend to see the adherents of these movements simply as 'bad people'. Their leaders' methods, from Trump's dog-whistle racism right through to Islamic State's mindless brutality, should not be excused. But inexcusable reactions are often the result of very real injustices. We cannot allow our condemnation of their methods to absolve us of the responsibility to work to fix the system that produced these monsters. To that end, I propose six principles for a responsible globalism that can, over time, win over a far greater part of the world's public. The fanatics will never be convinced, but their well of support can gradually be drained by a fairer vision of a more united world.

The first two principles deal with how we talk about ourselves as a global people. To start with, we need a truly inclusive definition of who 'we' are. We must stop using the vague term 'Western' as if it referred to white people, advanced economies, democracies and people that matter, all at the same time. This devilishly common syllogism creates a dangerous 'us and them' view of the world. Equally, as China rises, it must not fall into the same trap, attempting to build a global community on a model where ethnic Han (about the same proportion of humanity as so-called 'Westerners') are the only people who matter.

Having determined who we are, we need to be clear about what the global nation is for, and what it is against. Every country on earth has already signed up to an impressive set of Global Goals, demonstrating a common desire to promote human wellbeing and protect the planet. The challenge is to recast those goals from being a dry United Nations agreement to become a viscerally felt mission that people everywhere want to support. Even more imagination is required to ensure that the global nation's enemies are not people but the real threats to humanity, such as disease and climate change. Humans have frequently made such imaginative leaps to enable successful collaboration in bigger groups. We can do so again.

The next two principles are about what we need to protect so that the identities and institutions that people hold dear are not swept away or undermined. The nation-state, the most successful organizational unit that humans have ever created, should be maintained and strengthened as global cooperation spreads. Our 200 or so nation-states should keep as much autonomy as possible, constrained only by the imperative that they avoid harming each other.

Critically, that means protecting citizens' right to democratically control the level of immigration into their nation-state. Globalists have too often sought to ignore or undermine that democratic will. They should be confident that, over time, they will win the argument for greater mobility without the need to force it on an unwilling public.

The last two principles deal with the two areas in which we should push for the most radical change. A globalized economy stretched over a patchwork of independent tax jurisdictions has resulted in the wealthiest people and corporations simply choosing not to pay tax. Countries cannot solve this problem on their own. We need to demonstrate that a globalized world has the tools not only for the rich to get richer but also for governments to ensure they pay their fair share.

Finally, we should push for a more just geopolitical order. A global nation does not require a monolithic global government that interferes in everyone's affairs. It simply requires that the United Nations maintains a monopoly on the legitimate use of force. To improve global justice, we must ensure that our most important collective decisions, such as when to intervene in situations of conflict, are taken on a more inclusive basis.

These are not decisions that governments can take tomorrow. The political will for such reforms will not emerge until a social movement calling for a fairer, more united world has captured the imagination on every continent. This will not be the work of an election cycle, or even a generation. Creating a nation typically takes a hundred years to succeed, or indeed to fail, as many have. Success is not guaranteed, but the choices we make will determine whether the pendulum swings back towards a more collaborative world or crashes into the wall of populist anger.

Globalists and Nationalists

The world has become small not only on the map, but also in the minds of men. All around the world there are some ideas which millions and millions of men hold in common, almost as much as if they lived in the same town.

Wendell Willkie, *One World* (1943)

Globalists and nationalists are generally seen as sworn enemies. Globalists tend to stress the interdependence between countries, the benefits of close cooperation and the commonalities between all humans. Nationalists usually focus on the duty that citizens of each country have to each other. Neither position is inherently irrational but, as the political stakes of each have been raised, these terms have become at the same time badges of honour for one side of the debate and terms of abuse for the other.

The truth is that globalism and nationalism have far more in common than their respective champions like to admit. Nationalism as we know it is a thoroughly modern phenomenon. It arose in Europe in the late-eighteenth and nineteenth centuries and proved so successful that it was actively adopted across the world. It is based on the claim, embodied in the French Revolution, that all men are equal and should be governed by people who represent them, in their best interests. Nationalism was therefore an inclusive process far more than it was an exclusive one; its intention was to move from a position where the state was owned by a set of powerful monarchs and aristocrats with hereditary claims to one in which sovereignty lay with the people themselves.[1]

If the people were sovereign, precisely where did each sovereign people start and end? Nationalists argued that each state should embrace a natural grouping of humanity, known as a 'nation'.[2] This alignment between the nation (a natural grouping of people) and the state (the land and people controlled by a single government) would create nation-states – bundles of sovereignty, administration and collective will, stitched together by a common history and a shared destiny. This was the promise that made nationalists so popular as they conjured nation-states from the debris of empires, kingdoms and principalities on every continent.

Where to draw the boundaries of each nation was far from straightforward. Do the speakers of each language form a nation? If so, how to tell a distinct language from a mere change in dialect? What role should geography play? What of religion? Can a state turn its people into a coherent nation through policies of assimilation, or must we redraw the political map to align borders with existing cultural units?

Far from being narrow-minded, nationalists were often ambitious in defining their group. Bolivarian revolutionaries in South America and Arab nationalists in the Middle East and North Africa sought to create single nation-states for those who spoke the same language across huge geographical areas. Swiss and Yugoslavian nationalists sought to create nation-states for people living near to each other but divided by language and religion. Some, including many of the early leaders in the French Revolution, saw no boundaries to the nation other than humanity itself. The French National Assembly in the 1790s accepted members from any country, and the wars France waged between 1792 and 1815 were justified on the premise that all men should enjoy the freedoms they had arrogated to themselves.

The most inclusive versions of the nation failed not for want of ambition but in the harsh reality of implementation. Spanish South America ended up as nine separate states; the Arab 'nation' currently houses twenty-two; Switzerland held together while Yugoslavia did not. But where nation-states were successfully created they represented perhaps the most inclusive, egalitarian and emancipatory political development in history. Serfs were liberated, monarchs were unseated or constrained and the ancient privileges of the aristocracy fell away. In their place, entirely new conceptions of people and government were introduced. This was not always democratic but at least it claimed to be representative.

Nations created powerful stories and icons of common identity that tapped into deep wells of emotion in the human psyche. Perhaps for the first time in history it became commonplace for the mass of the population to be prepared to sacrifice their lives, if necessary, not for their family, village, lord or king but for the millions of other people represented by their nation. The significance of that change was highlighted by Goethe, who described the Battle of Valmy, which he personally witnessed in 1792, as heralding 'a new epoch in the history of the world'.[3] A ragtag French army had held off the better-trained and better-equipped Prussians, apparently due to their greater patriotism. The French were heard throughout the battle to shout '*Vive la Nation!*', the first time that an army had ever explicitly fought for that idea.[4]

The central charge against nationalism, then, that it is narrow-minded and exclusionary, is wrong. Nationalism is at its heart a project to bring people together in common cause. This is nowhere better summed up than in the life of the intellectual father of European nationalism, Giuseppe Mazzini, who was instrumental in the creation of the Italian nation-state but also inspired nationalist movements across the rest of Europe. For Mazzini, building the nation was merely the first step towards 'the universal association of the peoples'. He believed that 'every people is . . . bound to constitute itself a nation before it can occupy itself with the question of humanity'.[5]

Current nationalist movements can be just as inclusive. Scottish nationalists claim that the people of Scotland will benefit from no longer being part of the United Kingdom. They claim that their common history and a political consensus which is more left-leaning than that of England mean that they are a more natural unit of government as a separate state. Whatever the rights or wrongs of that argument, this is not an exclusionary or racist nationalism. There is no question of Muslim, Sikh or other ethnic-minority Scots being excluded from the new nation-state they are proposing to build. The Scottish government has a policy of welcoming immigrants (whom they call 'new Scots'), a school curriculum that emphasizes 'global citizenship', and has fought hard to keep Scotland inside the European Union.

We need to move away from the idea that nationalism is synonymous with anti-globalism, narrow-mindedness and racism. Historically, it is a scheme for uniting people by mapping modern government over the primeval human instinct to be an active member of a well-defined group. Nationalism has always left open the question of how broad that group can be. If the symbols of nationalism are being captured by anti-globalists, narrow-minded people and racists, we need to ask why.

And what of globalists? Are they merely rootless cosmopolitans with loyalty to no one but themselves? Certainly not the intellectual father of modern globalism, Immanuel Kant. Among his several propositions was that a single world government should be devised to ensure fairness and justice for all humans. But this globalist was a thoroughly rooted man who never once left his hometown of Königsberg. More importantly, he believed simultaneously in 'world patriotism and local patriotism', and said that 'both are required of the cosmopolitan'.[6]

Most globalists today are in the model of Kant. A broad social survey of 45,000 people in various countries reveals that the majority (56 per cent) of those who 'agree strongly' that they are 'citizens of the world' are also 'very proud' of their country.[7] By this measure, globalists displayed about the same level of patriotism as anti-globalists (of those who 'disagreed strongly' that they were 'citizens of the world', 58 per cent were 'very proud' of their country). The people who were least likely to be 'very proud' of their country were neither globalists nor anti-globalists but rather those who 'neither agreed nor disagreed' about global citizenship. Of them, only 35 per cent were 'very proud' of their country. This suggests that patriotism is not weakened by adding a layer of a globalist identity but rather by apathy about the world in general.

This result may sound strange at first, especially when set beside anti-globalist rhetoric. Theresa May famously told Britons that 'if you think you are a citizen of the world, you are a citizen of nowhere'.[8] How can it be that globalists are just as proud of their country as anti-globalists? Research into social cohesion bears out the finding. Political scientist Robert Putnam has shown that having an affinity with people from a wide range of groups increases the chances we will have relationships with people in our own group. For example, he found that, in the US, white people who have more non-white friends also tend to have more white friends.[9]

If we put aside contemporary political wrangling to think instead about the real people that we know, this makes sense. Are people who care most about the world uninterested in the state of their own country? Do people who give to international charities think it is wrong or unimportant to donate to local causes? Do people who have a strong sense of belonging to family or local community organizations ignore national politics and international affairs?

In my own life I have seen how local and international identities can reinforce each other. As I started out on my career, Iraq, the country of my father's birth, which I had never visited, was racked by civil war following the 2003 invasion. Moved by that tragedy, I decided to dedicate myself to trying to ameliorate conditions in the Middle East, focusing on education reform. But soon my thoughts turned to how I could use that experience to further social justice in the UK. Even now, my day job focuses on development in the Middle East, but I spend much of my spare time working on the school in North London that I co-founded alongside a group of other educationalists. My work abroad has increased both my ability and my desire to ensure that British children get a good education.

There is nothing unusual in my story. But sometimes globalists have internalized the criticism against us. One American philanthropy executive I interviewed for this book gave me a *mea culpa* – she felt that she and other internationally minded people were not sufficiently focused on local problems. As we continued our conversation, it emerged that she gave money to local charities, took an interest in local politics, would be happy to pay higher taxes and was an active member of her school's parent–teacher association. Not bad for a rootless cosmopolitan.

Instead of thinking of globalists as people who are devoid of any specific identity, we need to understand that they are as much prone to the tug of belonging as any nationalist. They are increasingly bound into a global community by the same forces that created nationalism. That has the potential to add another, powerful identity on top of the ones we already hold.

The idea of a single community of humankind is nothing new. A cosmopolitan strain of thinking has for more than 2,000 years suggested the possibility of all humans being part of a single community of citizens. Buddhism, beginning in the fifth century BC, was perhaps the first belief system to offer itself as universally applicable. In the Mediterranean basin, the first true cosmopolitans were the Romans, who were the first expanding state to welcome conquered peoples into their community on an equal footing as citizens. By 212, the Emperor Caracalla had granted Roman citizenship to every free man living in the empire, which, for its inhabitants, covered the great majority of the known world.[10] The mass religions which arose from the ashes of Rome – Christianity and Islam – inherited this cosmopolitan mindset. Unlike the place-based religions which came before them, they held out the promise for all humans to become part of the same community. Much later, Marxism offered a different kind of salvation, and unity, for all humans.

All these previous attempts to unify humanity have failed to do so because the conditions for success were not in place. Despite their powerful appeal, each came up against communities who refused to adopt their system and could not be forced to do so. Even among those who opted in, political unity could not be forever maintained.

These globalist schemes operated at a time when people and ideas circulated much more slowly and within a narrower radius. They used many of the tools that nationalism would adopt to create common feeling – a single uniting story, common symbols and rituals, the promise of a common destiny – but they were often too prescriptive to ensure universal adoption of the common identity which they proposed. Universal religions insist not only on the basic equality of humans but also that we worship the same god. Marxism requires not only that 'workers of the world unite' but also that they all agree that 'property is theft'. Nationalism holds so much uniting promise because it need not be prescriptive. Its only premise is that we believe we belong together.

Nationalism succeeded in reshaping society not just because it was a nice idea but also because four essential changes were taking place all over the world. These changes were brought about by the Industrial Revolution, meaning that nationalism spread alongside industrialized modernity, starting in Western Europe in the eighteenth century then moving through the rest of Europe and the Americas in the late-eighteenth and nineteenth centuries, and across Asia and Africa in the late-nineteenth and early-twentieth centuries as the conditions necessary for its success also spread. What is new in our era is that, since the late-twentieth century, these same four forces are now reorganizing societies on a truly global basis. That is increasingly creating the conditions for the idea of the global nation.

The first change is the spread of education. In pre-industrial societies, the vast majority of people worked in agriculture and were illiterate. They were born into their station in life and were not geographically or socially mobile. That allowed a small elite to rule over a diverse set of populations, each of which was rooted to its patch of land and did not partake in a shared national culture.

The tiny, literate, mobile elite often had an identity that was coterminous with the state itself, but this was not a national identity, as it was not shared with the majority of the people. Thus, for example, the educated elites of the pre-industrial Ottoman Empire frequently felt like Ottomans but most of the people they ruled did not.[11] They identified as Maronites or Muslims, Bulgars or Baghdadis, tribesmen or farmers.[12]

Even when there was no significant cultural difference between the rulers and the ruled, as in Russia, elites chose to create them.[13] The Russian Orthodox Church wrote its correspondence in an ancient Slavic language (Church Slavonic), which the common people could not understand, while the government of Tsar Peter the Great was conducted primarily in French.

Mass education changed this dynamic. As the economy diversified away from agriculture, there was a need for more people with a basic education. This created a reading public with more social mobility and whose cultural horizons were at least as broad as the state in which they lived, if not broader. Now that they were able to participate in high culture, they were far less likely than their rural ancestors to accept an entirely dislocated ruling elite.

Where mass education took off, nationalism followed. In Prussia, literacy rates rose from 15 per cent in 1770 to 40 per cent in 1830.[14] As we saw in the last chapter, this was the period during which the idea of a German nation changed from being something unthinkable to a concrete reality. In the Arab world, literacy and nationalism came much later. In the 1920s, when Arab nationalism was no more than a minority sport, literacy across the region was no more than 20 per cent, but between the 1920s and the 1950s school enrolment soared, creating a literate public.[15] The 1950s then saw a wave of nationalist sentiment that brought down governments in various Arab countries.

Today, education has spread globally. In 1970, three quarters of Nigerians, two fifths of Chinese and a third of Brazilians had received no schooling. Now, over 90 per cent of the world's children of primary-school age are in the classroom. As a result, the proportion of humans who can read and write has risen from just 42 per cent in 1960 to 85 per cent in 2014.

While education is most often delivered by individual nation-state governments, it is increasingly a global exercise. International league tables, such as PISA and TIMSS, are creating pressure for each country to learn from better performers, adopting their curricula and teaching methods.* This is not only a process that takes knowledge from rich countries to poor countries. Britain has adopted the Singaporean method of teaching mathematics.[16] Increasingly, there is a global standard of what people are expected to learn in mathematics, science and, crucially, language.

The second factor that prepared the ground for nationalism was the development, aided by the spread of education, of a common national language. We take for granted today that there is a single language called French, another called Russian, another called Japanese, and so on. But this was not the situation at the dawn of the Industrial Age. Agricultural societies, with their geographically rooted communities, had a proliferation of dialects, which blended

---

* PISA stands for the Programme for International Student Assessment, an initiative of the Organization for Economic Co-operation and Development (OECD) (http://www.oecd.org/pisa/). TIMSS stands for Trends in International Mathematics and Science Study, an initiative of the International Association for the Evaluation of Educational Achievement.

into each other as one travelled from village to village. This made drawing national boundaries even more arbitrary.[17]

Where mass education was remaking the minds of citizens, academics and bureaucrats were able to codify and promulgate a national language, normally based on the dialect of the culturally dominant group: Tuscan in Italy, Mandarin (literally, the 'language of the officials') in China, the Edo (Tokyo) dialect in Japan. Those dialects that did not attain the status of a national language would survive, at least at first, but were relegated to a subordinate position, excluded from literature, official business and polite society.

The creation of a single official language in which growing numbers of people were literate enabled the transformation of identity on the national level. This did not require universal adoption of the new lingo. In Italy at the dawn of nationalism, only 5 per cent of Italians are thought to have spoken what was to become their national language.[18] When nationalism gained traction in Germany in the early nineteenth century, there were less than half a million readers of the literary language out of a population of around 25 million.[19] But because these languages presented themselves as an indispensable route to advancement, they spread rapidly, bringing with them an increasingly unified identity.

India today presents an example of this process when only half complete. English, and increasingly Hindi, are official linguae francae that help to bind more educated Indians into a shared identity. However, pronounced linguistic diversity remains. It is not a surprise, then, that Indian national identity exists but is less pronounced than in many other countries.

Today, linguistic convergence is a worldwide phenomenon. English is now thought to be understood by around a quarter of all people. Almost as many speak Mandarin, but the role played by English is very different. Elites everywhere are expected to have at least a minimal grasp of English, as are those who work in service industries with an international clientele, from taxi drivers in major cities to workers in call centres. That is not just so that they can communicate with Americans, Brits or Australians. In a large proportion of global conversations conducted in English, none of the participants are native speakers.[20]

Even as the economic and political heft of English-speaking countries wanes, the appetite to learn English is holding up. That is because speaking the first-ever global lingua franca affords concrete advantages. The Chinese government ensures that basic English is mastered by every single one of the 9.4 million Chinese students who sit the Gaokao university-entrance examinations each year.[21]

This linguistic convergence is offering the possibility of a stronger globalist identity. Soon, technology may complete the trick. As Nicholas Ostler has argued, English is the first global language but might well be the last.[22] Artificial intelligence may soon allow us to communicate with anyone without learning a common language, as software seamlessly translates every language into our native tongue.

The third factor that powered nationalism was mass media. Now that they were literate, and increasingly shared a common language, the public in industrializing countries developed a ravenous appetite for the most advanced social media of the day – the newspaper. Thousands of printed copies of a single edition, made available simultaneously on a daily or weekly basis, allowed a wide range of people to take part in a shared narrative of unfolding events. In the history of every nationalist movement the emergence of newspapers is a central part of the story.

That does not mean that everyone read them. When the Italian nation was springing into being in the early nineteenth century, the biggest print runs of any edition were no greater than 10,000, in a population of 25 million. Even allowing for each printed copy to be read by (or read aloud to) many different people, it is unlikely that the reach of any article was ever more than a fraction of 1 per cent of the population.[23] All the same, from Italy to the Arab region, in India, across colonial Africa and Southeast Asia, newspapers drove nationalist sentiment.

In this regard, the global nation is already further along than Italy was 200 years ago. Most humans now have access to a globalized material and audiovisual culture. YouTube and Facebook each have around 2 billion regular active users (as of May 2018), having both nearly doubled their reach in five years.[24] Popular YouTube links can reach 1 billion views in a matter of weeks, which, even allowing that each person may have viewed the video more than once, means that perhaps upwards of 5 per cent of the human population has watched them.[25] Over 1 billion people – nearly 15 per cent of humanity – are thought to have watched the FIFA World Cup Final in 2018, up from less than 400 million in 2006.[26]

The conventional wisdom as I write is that widespread access to social media is simply replicating and even heightening social divisions by allowing its users to reside in self-reinforcing 'echo chambers'.[27] However, several recent studies have shown this to be a myth.[28] In democratizing and digitizing information, social media has not increased the polarization of politics or the prejudices of its users. Where politics has become more polarized, this is because of real differences of opinion as to how to move forward, especially following the global financial crisis of 2008. Social media, because we can watch it unfold in real time, has merely lifted the lid on the kind of polarization and misinformation that has always characterized public debate. Meanwhile, Russian attempts to influence US elections have shown that even nation-state political contests now operate on a global battlefield.

In fact, there is plenty of evidence of social media making debates more inclusive. One striking example is the #MeToo movement, a social-media-driven campaign against the sexual abuse of women that became a truly global phenomenon in 2017 and 2018. People I spoke to in China told me that this was the first campaign for social change originating outside the country to take on a meaningful and widespread presence in their country. For a global social movement to penetrate so deeply, even behind the 'Great Firewall of China', is a remarkable sign of the emergence of global cultural norms that transcend the imagined borders that we are frequently told separate different 'civilizations'.

The final factor that propelled nationalism was the circulation of a growing number of businesspeople, academics and bureaucrats. Most people never left the region in which they were born, but a highly mobile, educated elite became standard bearers of nationalist ideas which could then be communicated to the increasingly literate public through mass media.[29] The circulation of this growing, mobile class was powered by advances in transport technology, particularly the steam-powered railway. This started in Britain, with the first public passenger service operating between Stockton and Darlington in the North of England in 1825. What followed was a boom in mobility that transformed long-distance overland travel from being an expensive and time-consuming activity reserved for the extremely wealthy to a part of daily life for the middle classes.

Railway-passenger journeys in Britain rose from almost zero in 1840 to pass 100 million per year in the 1850s, reaching a remarkable 1.5 billion per year in the early 1900s.[30] Meanwhile, railways were built across Europe from the 1840s, in India from the 1850s, and across Latin America, China and Japan from the 1870s. Where networks of railways connected networks of thinkers, traders and officials, the national idea was greatly strengthened.

Recent years have seen just such an expansion in the globally mobile elite. It is 500 years since the first ship circumnavigated the world, but the current phase of economic globalization is by far the most extensive. Not only are there more international business-people than ever before, they represent a broader sweep of humanity. If early globalization was led almost exclusively by Europeans and colonists of European origin, that is no longer the case, as a glance across any airport lounge quickly reveals. While academia has always been a peripatetic profession, it is now truly global, especially since the opening up of formerly communist countries and the emergence of a new middle class in Africa and Asia. China is perhaps the most important example here, having been at the centre of both changes. Until the 1980s, its academics operated in near-total isolation from most other countries. By 2016, there were 4.6 million Chinese people either studying in or having already graduated from foreign universities, of whom nearly 500,000 had PhDs.[31]

We now also have a global bureaucracy of unprecedented scale. The first international non-governmental organization (NGO), the International Committee of the Red Cross, was founded in 1863, but since the Second World War the growth in NGOs has been astounding. In 1950, there were fewer than 1,000 active international NGOs, but by 1975 this had risen to 5,000 and there are now over 37,000.[32] The first truly global organization created by governments, the now-defunct League of Nations, was established only in 1920.[33] Now, there are around 5,000 inter-governmental organizations, of which 600 have been created since the turn of the millennium.[34]

The number of people employed or subcontracted by the UN and properly considered part of the UN's organizational culture is now probably between 1 million and 2 million people.[35] While there is some overlap between these people and the staff of other international governmental organizations (IGOs) and of international non-governmental organizations (INGOs), it is safe to assume that the total number of people working in global organizations, both IGOs and INGOs, is a multiple of this number – meaning that global bureaucracy now comfortably reaches the low millions of people.

That these people are circulating globally is thanks to the modern equivalent of the railway – air travel. Until the late twentieth century, international travel was as much the privilege of a wealthy few as an overground trip across the country was before the invention of the railway. But air travel has grown exponentially since 1970, from just 400 million passenger journeys per year in 1970 to 2 billion in 2005 and over 4 billion today.[36] Even allowing for an average of six international flights per traveller, that means that nearly one in ten people took an international flight last year.

All this shows that the monumental changes that happened within the territories we now call nation-states are for the first time operating on a global level. Previously, they transformed identities and led to a new political ideology – nationalism – which called for all the people within a territory to be treated as equal citizens under a government that represented them. It would be astonishing if the change of scale of these processes from being at the level of individual countries to being entirely global did not also create a powerful shift in the way people thought about themselves and their place within society. Such a shift is indeed happening. However, just like the first time round, the results are not predictable, nor is the passage to a new form of social solidarity likely to be smooth.

Many people will be unconvinced that a global nation is possible because, despite the undeniable spread of the forces I have described (education, linguistic convergence, mass media and mobility), in present-day politics the anti-globalists seem to have the upper hand. Much has been made of the rise of narrow-minded populists in recent elections. However, there is plenty of evidence of a strengthening globalist identity. The true picture is one of polarization, with more people flocking to each side of the argument and fewer sitting in the middle.

The most powerful data on national identity come from the International Social Survey Programme (ISSP), a periodic survey of 45,000 people in 33 countries across every continent – countries which together represent over one third of the world's population. The survey participants are broadly representative of the proportion of citizens at each education level and age bracket. The most recent ISSP data on national identity is from 2013, which was the first time a question on global citizenship was introduced.

The findings explode the idea that globalist identity is a small-scale, elitist phenomenon. When asked whether they agreed with the statement 'I feel more like a citizen of the world than of my own country', a quarter of respondents in the UK agreed or agreed strongly, rising to 28 per cent in the United States, 30 per cent in Japan and 36 per cent in Germany. But in India, where most respondents had limited education and wealth, fully 63 per cent said they were citizens of the world. In the Philippines, that figure was even higher, at 70 per cent. Overall, far more people in poorer countries evinced a globalist identity than in richer ones. Taking all countries together, the less well-educated respondents bought into global citizenship more than the better educated: nearly half of those with no formal schooling claimed to be global citizens, falling to 43 per cent for those who had completed primary education, and to just a quarter for those with a bachelor's degree. By weighting each country's results according to its population, the ISSP data implies that more than half of the world's population say they feel like global citizens.[37]

The ISSP survey does not include China, a country which is likely to increasingly shape global politics. However, the Globespan World Values Survey of 20,000 people in 2016, which asked exactly the same question on global citizenship, found that globalist feeling was even stronger in China than in India. The Globespan survey also shows us that globalist identity is rising worldwide. Having asked the same question about global citizenship in eight surveys since 2001, it found that in rich countries the proportion of positive responses has flatlined, falling slightly over fifteen years from 45 per cent to

42 per cent. But in developing countries, which represent the majority of the world's population, positive responses had surged from 44 per cent to 56 per cent in the same period. This change is likely to be driven by young people. A 2016 survey of 21,000 millennials in 186 countries found that they were most likely to define themselves as globalists, seeing themselves primarily as a 'human' (41 per cent of respondents) or a 'global citizen' (18.6 per cent). Self-definition as a citizen of their nation-state came a distant third.

Given the political climate, the flatlining of globalist identity in rich countries will not surprise anyone. But clearly something very powerful is happening in the developing world that is not being picked up by the narrative we are often fed. If 63 per cent of Indians and 70 per cent of Filipinos see themselves as citizens of the world, can it really be true that their popular elected leaders Narendra Modi and Rodrigo Duterte are part of the same phenomenon as Donald Trump, Alternative für Deutschland or the French Rassemblement National?[38] The answer, of course, is that they are totally different phenomena. Chinese, Indian and Filipino assertiveness are reflections of a stance that is less deferential to the old colonial powers but is resolutely outward looking.

Even Japan, a country which shares many social and economic features with Western Europe and North America, has not turned away from the world. Its government is trying to establish a more assertive role for Japan but is doing so by arguing for a bigger role in the UN. Japan has pressed ahead with trade deals and has even called for a global solidarity tax, paid for by financiers making foreign-exchange transactions, to finance international development.[39]

People in Europe and North America often have a blinkered view that globalist identity is dying because it is being challenged so forcefully in their part of the world. Those challenges are serious but, as we have seen, the idea of global citizenship is still on the march.

The United Nations and other traditional elements of the global system may be under threat from populist governments but the increased opportunities for collaboration thrown up by technology are allowing people to build new systems from the bottom up. Crypto-currency is a powerful example of this. Governments may not be willing to remove traditional forms of money from the control of nation-states, but that has not prevented the emergence of new, global forms of exchange.

Who are these masses of people that sign up to the identity of a global citizen? The truth is that the term covers a wide range of different perspectives and experiences. Most 'global citizens' in rich countries are university-educated, live in large, dynamic cities, travel abroad frequently and support their government giving foreign aid. They may feel part of a global movement, such as gender equality. Such people can be found in less wealthy countries like Nigeria, China and India, but there they are a tiny minority of people. So why do nearly two thirds of Indians say they are 'global citizens', even though most have limited education and have never travelled abroad? What is driving the less mobile and less educated Indians to see themselves as part of a global community?

It is the same factors that drove mass support for the idea of the nation when it first took hold. Despite not leaving India, they may well have migrated from the countryside to the city and become acquainted with a new set of people with different dialects and customs. They are likely to have relatives or friends who have travelled abroad and now send money back home. They may be aware of foreign investments producing jobs in their community, or perhaps foreign-aid projects from donors. With more disposable income than they had a generation ago, they use a range of foreign products, from toothpaste to fizzy drinks. All these things have engendered more awareness of the outside world and have brought a range of positive associations with them. But surely the most powerful force has been the spread of audiovisual media, which constantly presents them with stories and images from around the world.

These factors have deepened globalist identity for a huge portion of mankind. But it is important not to overestimate what this identity really means to people. Chinese academics I spoke to pointed out that the foreign students now studying at Chinese universities – a very recent phenomenon – have a very different experience than foreigners in American universities. They tend to be completely socially and physically isolated from the main body of students. This reflects a clear view that the Chinese-versus-foreigner identity is more important than their common identity as students. The same point is made more crudely by racist stereotypes of Africans on Chinese television programmes, which have portrayed people of colour in a way that was common in America in the mid-twentieth century but is seen as unacceptable there now.[40] Some may associate with the term 'global citizen' because it brings positive connotations but may not be living out the cosmopolitan values that many of us would associate with the term.

Two other questions in the ISSP survey are revealing. In addition to their sense of global citizenship, respondents were asked how much they agree that their country 'should follow its own interests even if that leads to conflict with other nations' and whether 'for certain problems, like environment pollution, international bodies should have the right to enforce solutions'.

In developing countries, where there was huge support for the idea of global citizenship, people were worryingly comfortable with conflict. Just 12 per cent in Turkey, 16 per cent in India, 27 per cent in South Africa and 40 per cent in the Philippines wanted their country to avoid conflict while pursuing its interests. This is understandable – in countries which have been less powerful over the past two centuries, the sense of belonging to a wider world is tempered by a determination to catch up with richer countries. Given the history of colonialism and conflict in many places, many people in developing countries expect that even pursuing their legitimate interests will lead to conflict. This forces us to temper our understanding of what 'global citizenship' means to people in those countries.

On the other hand, the responses on global-enforcement powers were surprisingly positive. A majority of respondents in every one of the thirty-three countries surveyed agreed that international bodies should be able to enforce solutions on issues like the environment. Weighting the responses by each country's population, ISSP indicates that just over two thirds of people worldwide support giving enforcement powers to international bodies. That is a remarkable result, given how difficult it has been politically to create binding international agreements. It indicates that, in some ways, the general public is more globalist than the governments which represent them.

Of course, such a simplistic question is easy to agree with in a survey. Designing enforcement mechanisms that do not leave the citizens of some countries feeling discriminated against is quite another matter. That is especially true when we consider how many people said they would be prepared to pursue their country's interests, even at the risk of conflict.

What we have, then, is a complex picture. We can dispense with the prevailing view in Europe and North America that globalism is dead. But how deeply ingrained this new identity is should not be overstated. A huge majority of people expressed support for at least one of the globalist identity measures I have discussed, either claiming to be a citizen of the world, wanting to avoid international conflict or supporting global enforcement. But the vast majority also have doubts about at least one of these ideas. In fact, weighting by country population, just over 5 per cent of the world (around 400 million people) supported all three measures of globalist identity.

Taking these results together, it appears that the world as a whole is in very much the same position as individual countries were at the dawn of nationalism. The economic and technological conditions for a unifying identity are in place but it has not yet coalesced in the minds of most people. Many attempts at creating national unity have failed. Others have succeeded at far too great a cost. Where nations have been built most effectively and with the least violence, it is because they have got three things right.

They have articulated an identity that is sufficiently inclusive to convince as many as possible of their prospective residents that they are part of the club and are on board with the mission. They have protected the existing institutions and identities which the people hold most dear so that the creation of the nation has not felt like the erasing of all that came before. They have presented a positive vision of how life will be better inside the new nation, pointing to concrete improvements that the national community will bring. Globalists must learn from this history and do the same.

Currently, globalist identity is not sufficiently inclusive. For too many people, it is synonymous with an imagined 'West' that is white, rich, democratic and capitalist. As Amartya Sen notes, 'the champions of this reading of history tend to feel upset . . . by the way the West's highly beneficial bestowal to the world is spurned and castigated by an ungrateful non-Western world'.[41] For as long as this confusion of 'global' with 'Western' continues, we can expect that angry reaction to grow. History has plenty of examples of national communities which have descended into violence because they have been cast in the image of just some of the people, to the exclusion of others.[42]

Today, there are two kinds of reaction to the narrative of 'Westernism'. One comes from a place of strength: increasingly powerful countries like India and China, which do not see themselves as 'Western', are asserting their independence from the 'Western' model. If globalism can be cast more broadly, this can become a debate about what kind of global community we want to create. If 'global' remains a synonym for 'Western', the risk is that competing spheres of influence emerge, to the danger of international peace and security. The other reaction comes from a position of weakness: some Muslims, feeling that the global system represents an attack on their identity, but without any obvious means to oppose it, have turned to random acts of violence as a form of generalized resistance.

Globalists have also done too little to show that they want to protect existing nation-state communities. In particular, globalism feels like a threat to many people in rich countries because globalists seem determined to fling open borders and destroy or at least weaken the nation-state. This is especially threatening to less educated people in richer countries, because their most valuable asset is their citizenship. By far the biggest factor determining the living standards of any randomly selected person is still the country in which they were born.[43] Being a low-skilled citizen of the United States allows you to earn around ten times as much as an equally skilled Nigerian.[44] In addition to earning power, citizens of rich democracies have the right to participate, through the electoral system, in setting the direction for the richest and most heavily armed institutions in the world – their governments.

Globalism has been presented as a grave threat to all these benefits. Floods of immigrants will compete for your job, which may itself be shipped overseas. Your vote will no longer count, because your government is bound by international treaties. Your wealthier fellow-citizens now care equally about all humans so do not expect any special favours. Steven Pinker provides a good example of the globalist attitude that can be seen as a callous disregard of fellow-citizens when he writes, 'It's true that the world's poor have gotten richer in part at the expense of the American lower-middle class, and if I were an American politician I would not publicly say that the trade off was worth it. But as citizens of the world, we have to say that the trade off is worth it.'[45]

With well-regarded American intellectuals espousing such sentiments, it is hardly surprising that many low-skilled Americans feel they have more to lose than to gain from globalism.

Last but not least, globalists have not been sufficiently clear about a positive agenda for change. Too often, they look like defenders of the status quo. We talk a lot about human rights, but it is not clear that we are prepared to address the world's deep economic and political injustices.

Despite unprecedented wealth creation, recent years have seen the long-term stagnation of incomes for both the very poorest people and lower-skilled people in rich countries. The share of income accruing to workers has fallen while wealth has become concentrated in the hands of a small number of people. Small and medium-sized economies, such as Greece and Argentina, have been exposed to destabilizing inflows and outflows of capital. These and other outcomes of structural problems in the global economy have caused much of the anger against globalization today. It is clear that various different approaches will be needed to address them but, to my mind, when viewing the world as a nation-in-waiting, one economic injustice stands out: the fact that the very richest people pay little or no tax.

The world's millionaires are simultaneously those who benefit the most from an advanced global economy and those most able to contribute to it. But we have done far more as a global community to create the circumstances for creating wealth than to build systems for ensuring fair taxation. That means that the burden of paying for nation-state governments, and of paying for the foreign aid that finances global development efforts, rests on the shoulders of those less well-off. This feeds the impression that globalism is no more than a conspiracy to make the rich richer on the backs of everyone else. Elections everywhere, from Britain to Brazil and from Pakistan to the Philippines, have been dominated in recent years by anger against an elite that seems to be enriching itself – often illegally – rather than contributing to the development of the country.

If economic injustice is a source of anger, political injustice is even more so. Major decisions in recent years – such as to invade Afghanistan and Iraq, to bomb Libya, Syria and Serbia, but not to intervene in genocides in Rwanda, Myanmar and the Central African Republic – have revealed time and again that the world system is, at its heart, a playground for bullies where the strongest get their way while the weak have little protection.

According to the current global system, these life-or-death decisions for thousands – even millions – of people, should be taken by the UN Security Council. The Security Council's rulings are decided for the most part by its veto-holding permanent members: the United States, Britain, France, Russia and China. That means that, even according to the current rules of the game, there is next to no representation for the vast majority of the world. Worse, events in Iraq, Syria, Georgia and Ukraine in recent years have shown that even the Security Council system, unfair as it might be, is liable to be ignored by powers intent on using their military might unilaterally. It is hard to overstate the anger that what seems like a hypocritical, or sometimes even shamelessly lawless, global security order creates among people who feel that they have been its victims.

All these failings – the failure to talk about ourselves inclusively, to persuade people that we will protect what they most value and to present a compelling vision of a better world – are holding back the development of a stronger globalist identity. The result is that we are still far away from the kind of political consensus that would allow concerted action on climate change, nuclear disarmament, poverty and disease. None of these challenges can be solved by countries operating on their own. Unless we succeed in inculcating a deeply held belief that all people belong to a single global community, our governments will never have sufficient incentive to work together.

That is why it is time for a new globalist credo. In the next chapters, I will present the six principles that I believe responsible globalists should stand behind if we are to begin the transition from a fractured world to a global nation.

Principle 1: Leave no one out

The vast association of the nation includes all the social elements and all the social forces.

Giuseppe Mazzini[1]

Like any national movement, globalists need to carefully define who belongs. At one level, this may seem obvious: it encompasses all humans on the planet. The line between 'in group' and 'out group' could not be more well defined, or justified. The same could not be said for other national projects. As nationalist leaders tried to identify the members of their nation in the nineteenth century, significant problems emerged in the many regions where languages and ethnicities existed side by side. In the early 1800s, in Kyiv, the future capital of Ukraine, Polish was the most common language. If you were from Kyiv, spoke both Polish and Ukrainian and your ancestry was unrecorded, which nation did you belong to? My family, living in northern Iraq, spoke Turkish and Arabic fluently and were of mixed descent. Were they Arabs or Turks? Naturally, given Iraq's establishment as an Arab state, they decided that they had been Arabs all along.

In today's world, the increased prevalence of dual citizenship raises a similar issue. The United States government grants visa-free entry to British citizens as an expression of the level of trust between the two nations. I am a British citizen born in London but, because I also hold Iraqi citizenship, I am excluded from this circle of trust. Since 2015, I am required to obtain a visa for entry into the US. Does the American government consider me to be part of the British nation? To some extent it does, but not entirely.

This uncertainty is mirrored at the level of personal identity. For the millions of children of immigrants such as myself, the challenge is not just that other people constantly ask us which country we are from. It is also that we are not quite sure of the answer ourselves. These numerous in-between cases point to the arbitrary and problematic nature of national self-definition, what philosopher Kwame Anthony Appiah calls one of the 'great mistakes about identity'.[2]

Defining our nation so as to include all humans would resolve much of this confusion, but not all. We need to avoid talking about the world as a dichotomy between the West and the rest, in the process driving a wedge between globalists in Europe and North America and the (even larger) number who live elsewhere. Instead, we should focus on building a set of inclusive narratives that tells the story of our commonality and destiny, learning from the incredible power of romantic nationalism.

The experience of nation-building in the past has shown that nations have struggled to define themselves not only with regard to faraway foreigners but also against 'internal others' who are seen to pose a threat to the national project. Such were Jews to the Nazis; such are Rohingya to Burmese nationalists in today's Myanmar. These internal others are within the nation, but not quite part of it.

Deprioritizing, or even entirely leaving out, significant sections of the population within a national narrative is, of course, morally wrong. Moreover, it risks creating a vicious cycle that undermines the success of the national project.

The modern history of Iraq is a good example. While Kurdish and Shi'ite elements were always acknowledged to be part of Iraq in the official telling, successive governments' prioritization of an Arab identity for the country fed Kurdish desires to break away. At the same time, many Shi'ite Arabs, constituting a majority of Iraq's population, saw a diminished role for themselves within a broader Arab community where Shi'ites were a small minority. While mostly seeking to retain the integrity of the Iraqi state, many have sought in recent decades to radically recast the identity of the nation, away from the vision of Arab nationalist leaders of the twentieth century. This rejection of the national narrative, by groups who felt deprioritized within it, led in turn to those groups being distrusted and further excluded. In the 1980s, as fears grew about the loyalty of Shi'ites, the Iraqi government began identifying on citizens' passports those who were considered to be of Iranian background and therefore not fully Iraqi. In this way, the de facto and even *de jure* unity of the nation was unpicked. Iraq's violent collapse since 2003 has provided the sad culmination of a century of nation building which failed to tell a sufficiently inclusive narrative of national identity.

For a global nation to succeed, we need to define ourselves in a way that leaves no one out. And yet many globalists talk about 'the West' as if it were the global 'in-group', to the exclusion of everyone else. For many authors, 'the West' is now used in place of what in the mid-twentieth century were routinely called 'civilized nations'.[3] Take, for instance, Bill Emmott's recent book *The Fate of the West*, which begins with these words: 'For as long as any of us can remember, to be modern has meant to be Western, and to be Western has meant being at the forefront of pretty much everything – of science, of social change, of culture, of affluence, of influence, of power in all its forms.'[4]

For others, the West means 'people that matter'. For example, the *Economist*, probably the most prominent mouthpiece for elite globalism, is clear that when there is a problem anywhere, the people who should act are 'the West'.[5]

To get a sense of what 'West' and 'Western' mean to the people I know, I asked as many as I could, both in person and through a call for input on social media. The most common answer was to make a list of countries. Some Middle Eastern respondents felt that Russia was part of 'the West', which effectively referred to 'white people'. To others, especially Americans, Russia was the antithesis of 'the West'. Someone even told me 'the West' was the Americas and did not include Europe. There was disagreement as to whether Australia fitted in. But most often the people being referred to were Europeans and their colonial diasporas, that is, people of European (sometimes only Western European) descent. There was great confusion as to whether an African-American or Latino-American was 'Western'. I was told that Japan might be considered to have become Western, but 'only in an ironic sense'.

Most revealing were the answers that defined 'the West' by some virtue or choice. Common definitions of the West included 'rich countries', 'developed countries' or 'democracies'. One senior finance executive told me 'The West means countries that have gone through the Enlightenment.' An American professor of government said: 'To me, the West is the idea that the state should be subordinated to the individual.' A friend related that his professor at Yale told him: 'The price of inclusion into the West is that you have to be critical of your own culture.' A minority view in my network was that the West was defined by vice rather than virtue: 'those who seek to impose liberal values on other regions', or simply, 'the white men running the world'.

So 'the West', this ubiquitous concept which is used constantly not only by people who feel they are part of it but even more so by those excluded from it, turns out to be a complex bundle. It not only refers to people of European descent but also denotes people who are more successful, morally superior and globally dominant. There is no question that for most 'Westerners', 'the West' is something that all people should aspire to. Some people will tell you that, if you try hard enough, you will be let into the club, but most agree that the best that those of non-European descent can do is to be 'Westernized'.

'Westernized' is perhaps one of the most unfortunate and politically charged words used today across the developing world to denote 'speaker of English', 'more educated', 'more intelligent', 'more trustworthy' and any number of other supposedly positive attributes. From my experience of working in the Middle East, Asia and Africa, it rarely occurs to foreigners that among the locals they meet there may not be a perfect correlation between their skill in English, their intelligence and their honesty. Of course, framing people in this way implicitly states that their essence is somewhere else. It indicates that their positive traits are a foreign appendage, in contrast to their inferior core. I have never heard of a European person who speaks Mandarin being said to have become 'Asianized'. They are just someone with a language skill. They are not seen as being on the path to any particular form of enlightenment.

The concept of a coherent 'Western' history, culture and viewpoint can be quite easily revealed as a fiction after no more than cursory examination. Not only are 'the West's' borders impossible to draw, not only is it geographically misnamed,[6] not only do its constituents – however defined – differ greatly from one another in political system, in culture, in viewpoint, more than this, the very building blocks of 'Western civilization' are imports from the supposedly barbarous East. Western culture, if one could be said to exist, must surely be seen as defined above all by Christianity, a Middle Eastern religion introduced by an emperor from the Balkans (Constantine the Great, who hailed from what is now Serbia), who ruled the lands from Britain to Syria from his palace in what is now a major city in Turkey (Constantinople, now Istanbul). This is just one of many possible examples to show that borrowing, exchange and ambiguity have more explanatory power than narratives of cultural exceptionalism.

However, the fact that 'the West' is a fiction is not the principal argument against it. All group identities are a fiction of sorts, and none more so than the idea of 'the nation'. The idea of a 'global nation' is a fiction which this book is energetically promoting. Rather, the case against Western exceptionalism is that it has serious negative consequences. Its use as a global in-group defined both by race and supposed virtues sets up a global community which prioritizes the dominant group in exactly the way that national projects have done in the past. We saw in the previous chapter that the majority of people who say they are global citizens in fact live outside the countries typically defined as 'Western'. These Nigerians and Indians and Arabs and Chinese want a more interconnected world and share many values and preferences which are supposedly 'Western'. But according to the 'West is best' narrative, they are not 'one of us' and must enter the global community in a subordinate position.

No wonder that China – huge, rapidly developing and confident – is working to create an alternative global system, one in which it can operate on its own terms.[7] No wonder that many Muslim communities in regions with low growth and insecurity are turning away from the global system and towards an escapist fantasy of past glories regained. Of course, these trends cannot be combatted by a narrative alone, but the idea that 'the West' is at the forefront of pretty much everything drives such communities further away from the idea of humanity progressing as a whole.

Globalists will never succeed in creating a unifying narrative as long as the idea of a Western 'in-group' is part of it. People of European origin need to give up the idea that there is something essentially 'Western' about some of the advancements that their ancestors gave the world. The use of paper, or gunpowder, is not seen as 'acting Chinese'. People who use writing or have legal codes or live in cities are not considered 'Iraqized', although all those things began in southern Iraq. Those who use alphabetic script are not thought of as adherents to the 'Lebanese way', despite every known alphabet in the world originating from Phoenician.

Going further back, agriculture was invented in a handful of different places – the Fertile Crescent in the Middle East, the Niger Delta in Africa, the Yellow and Yangtze river valleys in China, and in Mesoamerica. Those early agriculturalists spread this new lifestyle to nearly every community on the planet. They were not superior people in any deep or permanent sense, but they had some advances worth adopting.

Many inventions that happen to have been made in Europe or North America are in this category, from the light bulb to the personal computer. For others, such as liberal democracy, the debate as to its universal applicability is ongoing. But that debate is hampered by claiming that these ideas are inherently 'Western'. Amazingly, it is still common to talk about 'Western medicine', despite the fact that many advances are being made in Chinese labs, while 90 per cent of global vaccine production is in India.

The central concept of this book, that of 'the nation', is one that happens to have sprung up in Europe and North America but has shown itself to be universally useful. Although its early adoption was connected to the global dominance of Western Europe, it has been taken up by every state in the world, primarily because it is so helpful as a tool for overthrowing empires, establishing legitimacy in politics and spurring common action among citizens, not because it was 'Western' per se. Now that it is widespread, contemporary nationalism should not be thought of as a 'Western' or 'European' political form but rather as a global one.

While 'Western' is often seen as a synonym for 'global', other cultures are expected to remain local. There has been a growing tendency in recent years to insist that cultural production from outside Europe and North America should be somehow preserved exclusively for the group that made it. This argument states that the adoption by white people of cultural forms originating in India, say, or China or West Africa is wrong and constitutes a form of theft, or appropriation. For example, in the United States there was a recent uproar over a high-school student who is not of Chinese origin but wore a Chinese-style dress to her prom. Social media postings of her wearing the attire attracted wide-scale criticism from other Americans, some of Chinese origin, who felt that her actions 'appropriated' Chinese culture in an unreasonable way.[8]

The response from China, however, was instructive. As the controversy spilled out from American shores, thousands of people in mainland China publicized their support for the choice of prom dress, which they thought of as a compliment rather than an offence.[9] They had a point. Chinese people for decades have regularly worn clothes in a style which indicates significant borrowing from Europe and North America. They didn't feel that they were 'appropriating' European culture by doing so. Why shouldn't their fashions travel in the other direction?

It is necessarily true that the way cultural artefacts are used and spread will be deeply impacted by the relationships of power and wealth across human society. The fact that musical traditions that had been developed almost exclusively by African-Americans were popularized, and monetized, by white musicians such as Elvis Presley does reflect the deep unfairness that has characterized relationships between white people and people of colour in America. It is right to try to unpick that unfairness at source. It is also true that often in the past Chinese and other Asian and African fashions entered Europe and North America as the result of literal appropriation – theft – of palaces and cities by marauding soldiers and colonial administrators. But the answer is not to put every culture 'back in its box'. We should continue healthy and enjoyable cultural exchange while striving to do so as much as possible on a basis of equal respect and standing. A global culture is already forming – the most dangerous cultural theft would be to take away any artist's or community's right to contribute to the emerging whole.

Moreover, digging deeper into the way cultural production happens reveals the fallacy of an essentializing cultural project. That is because production does not tend to happen at the centre of cultural traditions so much as at the interstices between them. Borrowing, combining, reformulating and adapting inputs from outside – these are the basic steps through which all cultures have gone in order to produce their most characteristic forms. If a white American should not wear a Chinese dress, are all silk products now off the table? After all, the secrets of silk production are thought to have been smuggled into Europe from China by itinerant monks working for the Byzantine emperor Justinian in the sixth century AD. Should Van Gogh's works now be taken down from museum walls? His flat, patterned renditions of three-dimensional spaces were borrowed from Japanese art, which was highly fashionable in Europe in his time. Through this process of disentangling culture, we would be pulling at a thread that would soon unravel the entire tapestry and furthermore would rob future creatives of the nourishing impact of borrowing and exchange.

This argument is beautifully made by Kwame Anthony Appiah in *Cosmopolitanism*, in which he argues that cultural production is the property of humanity at large. He takes the instructive example of his own father's culture in the Asante region of Ghana. While regretting the British government's action in 1874, when it looted the entire collection of treasures owned by the then Asante king, he argues that, instead of restoring them to their previous home in Kumasi, a better solution would be for Britain to give back some of the major items, along with 'a decent collection of art from around the world', which would allow Ghanaians a broader cultural experience. He notes that the collection of the Asante king which the British took was not essentially Ghanaian but was 'splendidly cosmopolitan', itself containing items from Europe, Arabia, Persia and all over the African continent. Many of these items had themselves been taken by the Asante in war. Indeed, the original creation of the remarkable Asante collection is thought to have been inspired by the British Museum, the reports of which had impressed King Osei Bonsu in the early nineteenth century. In this sense, both the stolen artefacts and the London museum they ended up in reflect the same global system of cultural borrowing and production, albeit one shaped by historical injustice.

Globalists should be comfortable recognizing that, in an inter-connected world, the global goods we create are advances for humanity and the property of all (of course making allowances for time-limited intellectual-property rights for individual inventors). Hanging on to a 'Western' superiority, which is in truth a hangover from a racist and imperialist age, would be to repeat the mistake of countless nationalist movements in the past which have asserted the dominance of one part of the nation over the others with disastrous effect.

As China and India grow in economic and political power, there is equally a risk that people in those countries will seek to establish a similar 'us and them' view of the world. Hindus, and Han Chinese, are each approximately as numerous as 'Westerners'. A world view in which global unity must be achieved through the assimilation of all 'others' to the culture of one of those groups would be just as unhelpful a route as the one currently being attempted by 'Westernists'.

It is unclear what impact the growing power of China and India will have on global culture. Some people assume that the world will become more like traditional Chinese society.[10] I think this attitude betrays a fundamental error in understanding how and why cultures change. When Europe started to exert a massive influence on global culture, it was not traditional European culture that spread. Europe's cultural exports were recent innovations back at home – new technologies, new ways of organizing society, new ways of thinking about mankind and the universe. Modern Europe would have been as foreign to medieval Europeans as it was to those in other continents. If China or India radically reshape global culture, it will be because they have made comparably new and important shifts in their own societies, which others seek to adopt.[11] We should work to ensure that the next wave of innovation – whatever its source – is peacefully and voluntarily adopted, rather than being spread through imperial oppression, as European culture was in the past. For that to happen, we need to establish a much stronger global community, based on a unifying narrative for humanity.

How, then, can we think and talk about ourselves in a way that does not leave anyone out? Are we left with a tame universalism and a political correctness without passion? Must global culture be, in the words of Anthony Smith, 'historically shallow, memory-less . . .

demythologized and ambivalent ... value neutral and tradition-less'?[12] Again, the history of nationalism provides clues.

As national sentiment grew in long-standing states like England and France, it seemed obvious that membership of the nation should be defined as those living within the state's existing borders. This led to a non-ethnic view of nationality – minorities such as Bretons in France, or Huguenot immigrants in England, were part of the nation and would be assimilated over time into the great mass of the people, thanks to a strong state which could oversee the process. The same was true in the United States, where the newness of nearly all its inhabitants ensured a formulation in which the nation was defined by the extent of the government's authority and allegiance to that government was the only criterion of belonging. This idea of national identity is often called 'civic nationalism' because it derives member-ship of the nation from existing citizenship of the state. You are a citizen, therefore you are part of our nation.

As globalists think about belonging to the global nation, this approach has much in it that is appealing, because it welcomes the commingling of people from very different backgrounds, requiring only that they desire to be part of the national project. However, thinking about the global nation in this way would be a mistake. Naturally, there is no global state to which to belong. There is a global political order, exemplified by the United Nations General Assembly and Security Council. There is also a growing body of international law, backed up by international courts. But to make membership of the global nation contingent on support for these institutions would leave too many people out.

Globalists must escape the idea that their movement is about sup-porting the status quo. The existing global order is too weak, too anar-chic and too unjust to build an inclusive identity around. With loose coordination mechanisms papering over competing military alliances, it approximates a proto-state of the early-medieval European 'dark ages'. That is still a great advance on a world with no semblance of order, but it is not enough to win general support. In the near term, then, a civic globalism is divisive and inevitably creates an 'enemy within', consisting of those who refuse to sign up to an unfair global order.

Such a view of global belonging is also uninspiring. International institutions and international law are very important facets of the modern world, but they do not pull at the heartstrings of the average person. In Britain, civic nationalism entails loyalty to the Crown, a 1,000-year-old institution embodied in a single person, under whom generations of young men have fought and died for the safety and (more often) the expansion of the realm. Whatever one's view of the appropriateness of constitutional monarchy, there can be no denying that, as an institution, it pulls on the heartstrings of most British people. The same cannot be said for the office of Secretary-General of the United Nations. Too recent an invention, with too few glories to its name, no famous anthem, no Crown Jewels, its 'Buckingham Palace' an unremarkable office block in Manhattan, there is no chance that in the short term civic globalism will inspire the world.

There is another view of national identity, one which took hold outside the protective embrace of a state. The idea that the nation was not a fact of government to which people ought to adhere but rather a condition of the people to which government ought to adhere was first articulated by Johann Gottfried Herder, a German philosopher and student of that arch-cosmopolitan Immanuel Kant. Herder grew up in plucky, expansionist Prussia, which was just one of around 400 different states in Central Europe where German was a common language, although many other languages were also spoken in their territories. To Herder, the people to which he belonged were all 'Germans', part of the German nation, or *Volk*, which he defined linguistically. German speakers from the Rhine to the Black Sea, whether surrounded by other Germans or in small outlying communities, were all part of the indivisible German nation. The German nation, in turn, should unite and govern itself.

This became known as romantic nationalism, because it declared the eternal, undying existence of the nation, which was seen to have a single history, a single personality and temperament, and a single destiny. Herder believed that nations had been given these common personalities by the climate and the history which they had lived in and through. For him, language was the ultimate badge and carrier of this eternal unity, and wherever one language began and another ended, that was the natural boundary of the nation. A German was a German, whether they agreed with that fact or not. It was a question of culture and of destiny.

This romantic idea of the nation proved immensely powerful and inspired nationalist movements around the world which sought, and still seek, to redraw national boundaries in order to grant eternal nations the self-government they deserve. The unification of most (but not all) Italian speakers in the Kingdom of Italy and German speakers in the German Empire was a truly remarkable expression of the power of romantic nationalism, setting a precedent that others aimed to follow. In particular, Arab nationalists in the twentieth century were deeply influenced by Herder and the European unification movements which he inspired. Like German and Italian nationalists in the nineteenth century, Arab nationalists were struck by the weakness of their political and economic position with regard to Britain and France, whose combination of 'a people' and 'a government' in one seemingly organic whole contrasted markedly with the overlapping web of identity and government in the Middle East and North Africa. Over the course of the first half of the twentieth century, the concept of the eternal Arab nation, which should unify and govern itself, was to gain huge popular support, although its political aims were not realized.

Globalists are instinctively wary of romantic nationalism because of the many atrocities with which it is associated. Romantic nationalists in Turkey, Germany, Israel, India, Pakistan, Myanmar and elsewhere have attempted to 'cleanse' their surroundings of people who do not fit within their definition of the eternal nation. But while rejecting violence and persecution, globalists should learn from, adapt and apply romantic nationalism to their cause. Indeed, defining the global nation according to the framework of romantic nationalism is not only feasible, it is a necessary step towards building a functioning global community.

Claiming that *some* people constitute an undying nation that was culturally and even genetically superior to other people was a recipe for ethnic cleansing. But the claim that *all* humans belong to a single, interrelated family and ought to govern the entire planet is much less contentious. It does not exclude anyone. It sends a message to all people: you are one of us, whatever our differences. We may be divided, but we ought to be united.

So instead of trying to rally people around a set of imperfect institutions, we should focus on our shared humanity as the rationale for cooperation. Our common descent and our interdependent future in a depleting world can form a national 'myth' that is also unquestionable reality.

Romantic nationalism is so powerful that it has on many occasions driven many to lay down their lives in defence of that group, despite feeling little or no affinity to it just a few years previously. The remarkable speed with which it can take hold can be seen quite clearly in the case of Germans, Italians and Arabs to which I have just alluded. Civic nationalism in England and France is generally thought to have developed over a period of several hundred years, starting in the late-medieval period. Romantic nationalism, meanwhile, fired the imagination of millions in a matter of decades.

Yuval Noah Harari has brilliantly argued that building a successful society relies on creating myths which extrapolate the Palaeolithic groups in which we evolved onto a far larger community in which, by necessity, we do not all know each other personally.[13] Palaeolithic groups were very small, numbering probably no more than 150 members and frequently far fewer. Their members were highly related through intermarriage and therefore shared strong familial bonds. By necessity, each member communicated directly with all other members in a common language. The myth of romantic nationalism, then, imagines the nation as an extended Palaeolithic group: one ethnicity, imagined as a single group; one language, imagined as a single conversation; one species, imagined as a single family. Such is the nature of the human mind that, when successfully framed in this way, a common identity is not only plausible, it seems obvious and incontrovertible.

How, then, to articulate and promote a romantic globalism? The good news is that it is already starting to happen. The media is in a frenzy about populists who assert the separateness of their people, whether it is Donald Trump's 'America First', Viktor Orbán's 'illiberal democracy' or Narendra Modi's Hindu-centric vision of India. But this shouldn't allow us to ignore the amazing increase in people's willingness, and desire, to think and talk about humanity as a whole.

Start with the academic discipline of history. Nationalist movements have always rewritten history to demonstrate that their imagined nation was forever at the centre of events. In that context, one of the most extraordinary developments in recent years has been the explosion of the field of 'world history' from being almost non-existent in the middle of the last century to being a small but rapidly growing field from the 1980s onwards, and in recent years bursting out of the confines of academia into the bestseller lists worldwide.

Readers everywhere have developed a ravenous appetite for books about humanity as a whole. The most striking recent successes in this genre have been Yuval Noah Harari's *Sapiens* and its sequel, *Homo Deus*. These books are nothing more or less than the 'national' story of humanity. Harari does not, of course, stop at history. Like any good nationalist, he not only considers the nation's unified past (the focus of *Sapiens*), but also its common destiny (discussed in *Homo Deus*). And the readership is truly global. *Sapiens* was originally published in 2014 in Hebrew, a language with only 5 million native speakers, but by 2017 the English translation had sold over 1 million copies worldwide. In that year, both *Sapiens* and *Homo Deus* were among the top-ten bestsellers in China, demonstrating that the turn towards global narratives is by no means restricted to Europe and North America.

Just as earlier nationalist movements were propelled by a rapid increase in literacy, so, too, the global engagement in these stories has been aided by the further expansion of education. But it is neither realistic, nor necessary, that everyone buy a copy of the latest bestseller on world history. Romantic nationalism spreads through the dissemination of a new narrative into every form of culture.

This is happening today, in both high culture and mass media. High culture has always been the primary vehicle for spreading nationalism and it is playing the same role for globalism.[14] The BBC's most popular programmes in recent years include the television documentary *Civilisations* and Neil MacGregor's radio series *A History of the World in 100 Objects*, both of which aimed to weave human culture into a single narrative. Fine art, one of the most important means for producing cultural and ethnic identity, is increasingly a global medium, both in terms of its production and its reception. Going back in history, one can speak of European painting as communicating in a different 'language' to Chinese or West African painting. An expert in one tradition may feel they do not know how to 'read' works in the other traditions.[15] In the contemporary art world, however, to talk about European, Middle Eastern or Chinese art is merely to talk about specific conversations within a mutually intelligible language. In many respects, to break contemporary art down by country or region seems meaningless, or even impossible, given the extreme mobility and hybridity of its practitioners and their works.

This convergence of high culture is influencing what children are learning about their world. Countries as diverse as Scotland, Uganda, Colombia, Mongolia and Cambodia have 'global citizenship' as core parts of their school curricula.[16] But whether or not it is taught explicitly, the reframing of high culture as a global exploit is having an impact in classrooms all over the world. This steady realignment of perspectives is less newsworthy than the occasional decisions of education authorities to strike an anti-globalist tone, such as when the Texas school board decided in 2010 to require public-school students to study the threat global organizations such as the UN pose to American sovereignty.[17] But the increasingly global nature of educational curricula is probably the more important trend.

However, it is in the far broader arena of mass media that the battle over identities will be won or lost. In that noisier, more accessible realm, there are strong forces both for and against the global nation. On social media, content featuring every kind of prejudice is disseminated, sometimes by groups with a determinedly divisive agenda. Some of this content has been shockingly successful, even being shared by the US President.[18] And yet an inclusive human narrative is also being shared. To take an example, Nuseir Yassin, a Palestinian Israeli video blogger, has 9 million followers from around the world for his Facebook page, *Nas Daily*. Every day he uploads a one-minute video in English about a different country or community celebrating their culture. A strong theme throughout has been the common humanity of all people, including those on different sides of political conflicts. Yassin has made much of his comfort and even pride in a DNA test that shows he has some European Jewish ancestry. He and the many thousands of positive social-media activists like him are not shocking enough to dominate the headlines but they are popular with a wide audience.

Meanwhile, in the music industry, the latest creation from Simon Fuller – the talent agent who created the Spice Girls – is Now United, a pop group with fourteen members, each from a different country, representing every region of the world.[19] The consumption of popular music has been truly global for at least a generation. But for the product itself to be so consciously telling an inclusive human story is something new.

Probably the most powerful medium of all is that of film and television. There is much to despair about here. Movies like *American Sniper* project the martial valour of one set of people against a backdrop of dehumanized 'others' whose only purpose is to be killed. Series like *Homeland* present crude stereotypes in a Manichean world of good guys and bad guys. American dominance of the global film and television industry means that audiences everywhere are exposed to exactly the narrative which I argued above is so destructive to global unity: one in which 'the West', with America at its centre, is the unique moral authority and the only source of agency.

The single unifying story of humanity, so popular in history departments, high-brow documentaries and podcasts, has rarely translated into box-office hits.[20] To get a perspective on why that is, and what can be done, I spoke to Riz Ahmed, a British-Pakistani actor and rapper who has spent much of his life and career, as I have, engaging with questions of identity and how to build more inclusive narratives. With the bluntness typical of our long friendship, Riz told me that I hadn't found the human 'national story' because I was looking for the wrong thing. While telling a story so ancient that it captured mankind as a single community isn't impossible, he told me, it risks alienating viewers because it would be too general.

Riz believes that producing a strong sense of our common humanity is best achieved by telling individual, highly specific stories in which a wide audience can see themselves. These stories should be individually specific but collectively diverse, so that any one viewer is presented at different times with narratives set in a range of places and periods and through them is asked to empathize with people who at first might seem quite alien. Modern acting theory is based on the premise that the human experience is essentially the same for everyone, differing only in terms of the situation that different people are placed in. If they can succeed in imagining themselves in a character's true context, actors are told, they should, in theory, be able to play any part.[21] Successful storytelling, then, brings that insight to the audience: if you were in this person's shoes, you might feel the same as they do.

According to this view, diversity and eclecticism in film and television is enough to help people imagine themselves as part of mankind and not only some subset of it. As long as we can escape from the dull monotony of mono-ethnic, mono-cultural casting – particularly for the most empathetic roles – and move beyond the dehumanizing jingoism of releases like *American Sniper*, we will have done enough.

The global nation may not have an anthem and a flag, but it already has an increasingly captivating story which tells us who we are and where we are from. That does not stop at our last common ancestors 50,000 years ago. Throughout history, there have been figures whose contribution has been to urge for unity. These are the heroes, theirs are the narratives of the global nation. Not Julius Caesar, but Diogenes the Cynic, who was the first to declare himself a 'citizen of the world'. Not Kaiser Wilhelm, but Immanuel Kant, the great cosmopolitan philosopher who argued for a single world government. Add to the list all the inventors and thinkers who contributed to the cumulative sum of human knowledge, and those from every place on Earth who have argued for a somewhat broader view of who we are. It may be some time before the Secretary-General of the United Nations provides us with a heroic model powerful enough to stir the blood. But we are already starting to weave an inclusive, romantic story of who we are as humans.

Principle 2: Define the mission, and the enemy

A Nation is a living mission.
> – Giuseppe Mazzini, Letter to Mr Conway,
> 30 October 1865

We are resolved to free the human race from the tyranny of poverty and want and to heal and secure our planet.
> – Declaration of the United Nations Global
> Goals, 2015 (signed by the governments
> of all 193 member states)[1]

An essential element of the romantic idea of the nation that has been so powerful in uniting strangers is a clear view of its mission: what is it for, and what (or whom) is it against? It is this pivot from defining membership of a group to urging the group to action that provides nationalism with its most potent force. Channelled wisely, it has provided the political will for some of our greatest achievements. Misused, it has led to our greatest catastrophes.

Uniting masses of people in nationalist feeling and pointing them at a target is the political equivalent of splitting the atom. It can be used to create clean energy or to wipe out a city. If nationalism of the past can be compared with nuclear fission, globalism is like nuclear fusion: a far more powerful reaction. It is worth pursuing if you believe – as proponents of nuclear energy do – that the status quo is unsustainable and that we need to harness new forces to overcome our most important challenges. But given the complex history of nationalism, it is crucial to be alive to the risks – most of all, the risk that we turn on each other. How we define the mission, and the enemy, is of paramount importance.

Identifying the mission of the global nation should be relatively easy. Every government on earth has already signed up to a set of seventeen 'Global Goals', from ending war and hunger to ensuring gender equality and protecting the environment.[2] Each goal has a set of specific targets to be reached by 2030. This gives the lie to the view that the world is comprised of such radically different cultures that each has a totally different vision of what they value and what they want to achieve. Of course, there are cultural differences, as well as differences in strategic interests, among the various communities that make up humanity. But the hard work of negotiation to figure out the things we all agree on has been done over the last decade, in a mammoth diplomatic process with input from every government and many different sections of society.

It is striking how much consensus emerged. The Global Goals were not voted on by a worldwide referendum. We can be sure that some people in some places would disagree with one or another of them. But for all 193 governments representing every member of the United Nations to sign off on a single set of goals for the world is nevertheless an enormous and unprecedented leap forward in establishing common ground.

So we already have a mission statement for the world. The problem is that it is not yet embedded in the hearts and minds of most people, even globalists. Few people see the UN's Global Goals as a solemn pact that speaks to their identity and binds them to their fellow man in common action. They remain a political statement by governments, not a national mission for mankind. A survey in 2016, just one year after the goals were launched, showed that over a quarter of people worldwide knew about them, ranging from as few as 16 per cent of Russian and 19 per cent of Germans, to as many as 39 per cent of Indonesians and 44 per cent of Indians.[3] That is an impressive level of awareness for a new international agreement. But awareness is not the same as passion.

While the Global Goals represent a good candidate for a global national mission, other potential globalist projects might lead to disaster. For example, many globalists might get behind the mission to create a borderless world with unrestricted movement of people. But a nation's mission can only effectively unite its people if it represents a consensus. We are far from a consensus on free movement. Even more importantly, we must avoid uniting against any broadly defined groups of people. Too often in the past, nations have defined their mission through their enemies. Avoiding that trap requires a leap of imagination to manage and contain the demons of human nature.

Historically, nationalists have tended to define their nation's mission in two ways. Sometimes they justify action because it represents a positive ambition that is central to their identity as a nation – what the nation is *for*. Other action is justified because it removes a threat to the nation's survival – what the nation is *against*.

Let us look first at action based on what the nation is for. In many countries, ideas have made the leap from being technical government policies to becoming a major part of national identity. Such is health care in the UK. In 1948, Britain became the first country in the world to implement universal health coverage, through its National Health Service (NHS), as part of a range of measures that introduced the social protections collectively known as the Welfare State. The NHS's subsequent achievements in improving the health of the population and the model's replication in other countries have become an important part of the national story for British people and core to their identity – so much so that a majority of British people say the NHS is the one thing that makes them most proud to be British.[4] It would be hard to imagine many other countries showcasing their ministry of health as a centrepiece of the opening ceremony when they host the Olympic Games. Other nations have their own shibboleths. In the United States both freedom of speech and the right to bear arms fall into this category. In Japan pride in cleanliness is a deep-seated part of national identity.[5]

These national missions are not primarily questions of survival. They describe what the nation is *for* because they reflect a desire to create a better society that accords with the values of the national community. While they tend to present themselves as eternal, these national missions can change. Before the Second World War, it was arguably Empire, more than health care, that summed up Britain's national mission.

There is hope, then, that we can build up the Global Goals to be a truly universal project that people are prepared to stand for not because our survival depends on it but because it reflects our values as humans. This is where the opportunity lies for a global nation to put an end to much of the world's suffering by ending extreme poverty, tackling preventable diseases and ensuring access to human rights for all people.[6] The continuance of this kind of suffering does not present a clear and present danger to humanity at large, just as Britain's survival did not necessitate the NHS. Humans have muddled through with disease and inequality in the past and could just as well continue to do so. Rather, the appeal of the mission to support the most vulnerable people worldwide is that it speaks to the kind of world we want to live in and the duty we owe one another.

There is already one great example of a growing sense of globalist identity creating this kind of global mission, and that is the anti-slavery movement of the late-eighteenth and the nineteenth centuries. Not by coincidence, it arose at the same time as nationalism. Both movements were seeded in the soil of increased travel, learning and communication which allowed people to imagine a much wider fraternity of mankind than in the past. The voices of those former slaves who were literate and could publish and travel had a crucial role. One of the most prominent, Frederick Douglass, saw the power of the new medium of photography to break down stereotypes and communicate a shared humanity. He is said to have been the most photographed American of the nineteenth century.[7]

For anti-slavery campaigners, the fact of a common humanity was an important bond that established a minimum of mutual obligations between all people, thus representing a looser version of the kind of social contract that binds together a nation. While not implying a single government or the sharing of resources, this social contract for humanity made bondage and forced labour unacceptable and, importantly, made them unacceptable not only in their own country, but everywhere. An international humanitarian movement was born that insisted on this universal human right.

So where are we now? How near are we to the possibility of a globalist identity that stands for a real social contract for all people? For wealthier countries, one of the strongest pieces of evidence in this domain is the level of public support for foreign aid. This is the tax-payer money that wealthier countries send abroad to support other governments and people, whether to provide services like health and education, spur the economy or plug holes in public finances.

The basic operating principle of the nation-state, as formulated in the age of nationalism, is that part of the nation's wealth should be pooled through taxes to finance a government which will spend that money to ensure the safety and basic comforts of the group. How to explain foreign aid, where this pooled money is given to help foreigners?

There are three rationales which are normally used. Firstly, the money might need to be spent overseas to advance the self-interest of the donor country, for example if aid given towards assuaging the civil war in Syria is expected to reduce the likelihood of a terrorist attack in the donor country. Secondly, the money might be given as a one-off act of kindness due to extreme suffering, for example if there is a particularly destructive hurricane in the Philippines which touches people to make an exceptional donation. These two rationales accord with the traditional view of a world made up of many nation-states that do not have ongoing obligations to each other.

However, the third rationale for giving foreign aid is that, in a world of plenty, it is unacceptable for anyone to live in extreme poverty or die of preventable diseases. This explanation tends towards the view of humanity as a single nation. It builds on the centuries-old anti-slavery movement but goes beyond the idea that it is wrong for humans to be treated appallingly badly – more than that, it sees richer communities as having an active duty to pool their money into a system that provides for every human. This is not a question of self-preservation or even self-interest. Rather, it is about who we are as people. Support for foreign aid according to this globalist rationale can be seen as the first step towards a universal social contract for humanity.

A review of aid programmes indicates that decision-makers do buy into the view of foreign aid as a global social contract. Only 10 per cent of aid goes on humanitarian crises.[8] It is hard to argue that all the rest is designed to further the donors' self-interest. Major European donors have most often claimed that their aid is self-interested in two ways: firstly, that beneficiaries are less likely to migrate to the donor countries; and secondly, that violent extremism is likely to be reduced. But these arguments hold little water. In fact, the opposite is likely to be true.

Take immigration. Publicly giving money to help a poor community is about as good a way as any to send them a message that you are wealthier than them and life in your country is therefore likely to be more comfortable. If the development programme works, as people are lifted from extreme poverty they are more likely to migrate. That is why illegal immigration into Europe from Syria and Iraq, both middle-income countries, has been so much higher in recent years than from Yemen or the Democratic Republic of Congo, much poorer countries, which have also been ravaged by war.[9]

So much for aid reducing immigration. What about violent extremism? People who are lifted above subsistence levels and no longer spend so much of their time trying to ensure they have enough food for their next meal have more opportunity to engage in debates and organize themselves. In a world which continues to exhibit so much injustice, both in the form of daily conflict and through the structural unfairness of the global system, it is reasonable to expect that some proportion of that group of people reaching just over the $1.90 per day income level may be more, not less, likely to organize themselves against what they see as the pillars of an unjust global system. Violent extremism may go up, not down. Very few terrorists in recent years have come from absolute poverty. Like those who have joined violent political movements throughout history, they are more likely to come from relatively comfortable backgrounds while seeing themselves as part of a larger community which they believe to be subject to intolerable injustice.

Foreign aid that is paid on condition of the recipient government helping to erect barriers to migration, or which builds the recipient government's ability to target extremists, can be seen as directly following the self-interest arguments above. And European donors do spend money on such programmes. But much of their aid – thankfully – goes towards trying to improve the lives of the citizens of the recipient countries. The argument that this attains the self-interest goals described above is flimsy at best.[10]

This indicates that much foreign aid is spent to advance a globalist social contract. Is this a case of betrayal by 'Davos man' of an unsuspecting public? Not quite. It is regrettable that politicians often use unconvincing rationales of self-interest which they hope will reduce opposition to foreign aid from the sceptics. But the primary impetus for donors' aid programmes comes as a political response to the demands of the section of society that supports foreign aid. This pro-aid constituency generally shares decision-makers' cosmopolitan attitude.[11] In other words, governments spend some of their resources on creating a globalist social contract because many of their constituents want them to.

We should not overstate how well developed this globalist social contract has become. Citizens in donor countries are content to see between a quarter and a half of their country's total annual income given to the government in tax for redistribution within the nation-state. But even the most generous donor countries give little over 1 per cent of their annual income to foreign aid. The United States gives less than a quarter of 1 per cent. Supporting this relatively small contribution does not imply fully-fledged support for a global nation. However, it does represent progress towards that goal.

To strengthen the idea of the Global Goals as a national mission we need to make two major shifts. We need to think very differently about the project to help the world's disadvantaged people (usually referred to as 'global development'). And we need to change the way it is funded, transferring the moral obligation to pay from rich countries to rich people.

How to rethink global development? Again, nationalism provides clues. If supporting the most vulnerable people is what the global nation is *for*, it needs to be built on a positive story of achievement, not a narrative of doom and gloom. The British care about the NHS because they believe it has been a success. Americans care about freedom of speech because they believe their country to be the freeest on earth. Japanese people care about cleanliness because they enjoy living in a clean country.

The case for alleviating global poverty is normally made as an appeal to the heart, through images of starving, sick or otherwise miserable people who require help. We are all familiar with the image of a malnourished African child with flies buzzing around their face. Clearly, this approach can be effective as tug on the heart-strings that can spur action. But it also has many problems.

The constant presentation of a negative picture of human suffering suggests that the problems we have been throwing money at for decades are not being solved. Today, most people believe that global poverty is getting worse, not better.[12] This impression is both wrong and damaging. Less than half as many people are in absolute poverty now as in 1990, despite rapid population growth. The number of children dying of infectious diseases has also dropped by half. More people are being educated, more have access to power and there are more women in the workforce than ever before.

It is often countered that these improvements are all down to China's adoption of market capitalism, but that is not true. China is of course a big part of the story of global poverty reduction, but so are Ethiopia, Bangladesh, Indonesia and many other aid-receiving countries. Even in the Middle East, a region racked by wars in recent decades, there have been big improvements in health and education.[13] The narrative that the world is getting worse is not only false, it encourages the notion that foreign aid is a waste of money.

The exclusive focus on intense suffering in narratives of foreign aid is also problematic because it inspires sympathy but not empathy. National solidarity was created by the realization (or myth) of similarity, not difference. Traditional narratives of global development reinforce the perception that the poorest people are from another planet, sometimes even referred to as the Third *World*. The exclusive presentation of poorer parts of the world as characterized primarily by suffering is a source of great annoyance to many people from those places, who would like to establish a common experience and present a more nuanced view of their country.

How to tell a more positive story? That is precisely the task Richard Curtis, a renowned British film director (*Four Weddings and a Funeral, Notting Hill, Bridget Jones's Diary, Love Actually*), has set himself. In 1985 Curtis founded Comic Relief, one of the most successful public fundraising initiatives of all time.[14] In 2015 he launched Project Everyone, a campaigning organization dedicated to increasing awareness about the Global Goals. One early success was getting a highly creative one-minute commercial about the goals into cinemas in thirty-five countries, reaching 100 million people on the big screen. One third still remembered the commercial a week later after watching it just once – demonstrating an unheard-of level of retention for a cinema commercial.[15]

But long-term success in embedding the Global Goals in people's hearts and minds will require us to reach young people in a far more active way while they are still forming their views about the world. The World's Largest Lesson, also led by Project Everyone, alongside UNICEF, is an attempt to do exactly that. It provides resources and encouragement to schools all over the world to teach engaging lessons about one or more of the goals. In 2018, according to Project Everyone, 8 million children in 153 countries learned about the Global Goals by participating in the World's Largest Lesson, a 60 per cent increase on the year before. Between 2017 and 2018, around 1 per cent of all school-aged children took part.

It's a start, but it's not nearly enough. People who care about global action should be demanding that the World's Largest Lesson, or similar resources, are a compulsory part of their country's curriculum. After all, every government signed up to the goals in 2015. It is surely not too much to ask them to inform our children about what they pledged to achieve. The mission of every nation has been instilled in its people in the classroom. Putting the Global Goals on every curriculum would be a huge leap forward for the global nation. When I caught up with Richard Curtis, he agreed that creating a global nation was precisely the point of the exercise. He sees his job as 'finding the hits' – identifying those elements within the Global Goals that are most likely to speak to people's everyday reality and presenting them simply and beautifully to as many people as possible.

To change the narrative of global development we must also change the way it is financed. Change is already afoot. The remaking of the world economy over the last thirty years has greatly expanded the importance of donor countries in Asia and Latin America, such as China, Arab Gulf countries, South Korea, Turkey and Brazil. These emerging-market donors now account for at least 15 per cent of global aid flows, up from perhaps as little as 3 per cent in 2000.[16]

Emerging-market donors have a very different history and self-perception than donors in Europe and North America. Because they continue to have more poverty at home, they are more likely to insist on tying their aid to their self-interest. Because they were not the primary architects of the main global development institutions (such as the United Nations, the World Bank and the World Health Organization), they channel less of their aid through them. Because they often see their donations as an economic pact between peers rather than a 'civilizing mission', they frequently do not attach as many conditions to their aid. Emerging-market donors often have significant weaknesses in their own institutions.

Given these differences, they are often portrayed as presenting a threat to the global system. Why should poor countries carry out institutional reforms if they can reject European aid and turn to China? This attitude is mistaken. Emerging-market donors have increased the volume of resources available for global development. More importantly, their emergence means a massive increase in the proportion of humanity that is participating, through their governments, in global development efforts. That has to be a good thing.

Rather than a few very rich countries helping a few very poor countries, global development is now an arena in which almost every country is playing a part, whether as a donor, a recipient, or just occasionally as both (India, for example, both receives and donates foreign aid). To use the analogy of the nation-state, whereby aid is a rudimentary form of taxation to pay for basic welfare for the most needy, there are now far more 'taxpayers' with a stake in the global nation. For now, that system is complex, messy and contentious, with as much competition as collaboration (unable to secure more voting rights in the US-based multilateral bodies, China is busily creating its own). But if major conflicts can be avoided, there is an opportunity to create something far more effective than the old way of doing things. It is naturally uncomfortable for European and North American donor countries to see their influence being diluted in favour of other regions, but that process is both a symptom of a more equal world and a necessary step towards truly concerted global action.

However, the financing of global development should change still further. We have entered a phase of economic globalization in which the benefits are increasingly accruing not to individual countries but to individual people. That has produced a crop of super-rich in every country and undermined the historical privileges of the average citizen in wealthy states. In that context, it is increasingly unsustainable to expect the taxes of lower-skilled Americans or Europeans, whose own incomes have stagnated, to fund development programmes in poor countries, while millionaires from those countries contribute nothing.

My proposed approach, as articulated in Chapter 7, is the imposition of a compulsory minimum tax on personal wealth over $1 million, calculated at 0.5 per cent. Every jurisdiction would collect its own millionaires' wealth tax and spend it on whatever it wished. But out of the amount collected, each jurisdiction would be expected to contribute half (i.e. 0.25 per cent of personal wealth above $1 million) towards global development. As with current foreign-aid spending, this contribution would be voluntary but could be encouraged by tying its payment to each country's weight in voting at the United Nations.

Such a step would be transformative, casting global development as a universal project financed by the wealthy people in every country – those who are benefitting most from the globalized economy. Like most of the recommendations in this book, it is not something I expect to happen overnight. But as attitudes towards our place in the world and our duties to each other are reshaped over the coming years, there is an opportunity, if we push for it, to build a social movement for such a radical change.

Of course, for a mission to be universal, it is not enough that the wealthiest people contribute. Less wealthy people – who are far more numerous – must also be agents of such a mission, not just the objects of its attention. For the most part, this does not present great difficulties. People, on the whole, want to be healthier, better educated, less poor. Distributing malaria bed nets is manifestly a good thing – no one wants to get malaria. But one particular Global Goal is far more contentious than the others in this regard, and that is Goal 5: Gender Equality.

While every country in the world may have signed up to the goal, efforts to ensure gender equality are suspected by many communities to represent an attempt by foreigners to export their way of life and implant it thoughtlessly into other people's homes. In such communities, hostility to interference with gender relations often extends to women as well as men, begging the question: to what extent can we seek to empower people against their own will?

It is worth noting that the view of gender equality programmes as essentially exporting culture from donor countries to beneficiary countries is part of the reason for their popularity in donor countries. Many people in rich countries like the idea of aid that teaches foreigners to be more like them. In this way, it taps into that rich vein of pride that springs from a mission based on historical achievements: 'We have improved gender relations in our country, and are better for it; now we will help you do the same.' But this approach can be deeply offensive to those in aid-receiving countries.

This does not mean that gender equality should be excluded from the mission statement. It is too important a goal, promising a better life for too much of humanity, for us to consider setting it aside. Indeed, the great achievement of 193 countries publicly signing up to gender equality should be built on by cementing it at the heart of what we feel our global community is for. But we do need to proceed with a great deal of humility. That means acknowledging how recent and incomplete are the advances made by women in those countries who are closest to the forefront of the movement. It also means ensuring that the views and aspirations of local people in aid-receiving countries are taken into account at every stage. Above all, it requires patience. Cultural changes such as this take time.

If we can rethink global development in these ways, we have a chance to create a truly unifying story about what humanity is for. That story must rip up the rule book that seeks to contrast African or Asian suffering with European and North American saviours. We should think instead about a flatter world composed of people who increasingly live, and think, in similar ways, where it is the duty of the wealthy to ensure a basic standard of living for everyone.

Whatever we stand for, the surest way to inspire action is by focusing on what we are *against*. Millions of years of evolution have ensured that the survival instinct trumps pretty much any other motivation. That is why projects to unify people within a nation have so often called upon the urgency of a real, or imagined, survival threat.

Most often, the uniting threat has been that of foreign armies.

German and Italian national unification movements were propelled by the military dominance of France and, especially, the experience of Napoleon's invasions. Chinese and Japanese nationalist movements were given impetus by the threat posed by European and American 'gunboat diplomacy'. Arab nationalism was conceived as a rallying cry against imperialism and the loss of land to Israel.

This way of thinking is perhaps the biggest danger presented by the national idea. Before nationalism, warfare often did not stir the blood of the majority of the population, who, after all, felt little connection with the state. If they could survive the violence and looting, they frequently did not much care which side won. But in the age of nationalism, where the state was seen as an emanation of the people, protecting it became a sacred duty. That explains the unprecedented mass mobilization of soldiers, many of them signing up voluntarily, in the last two centuries. Indeed, nationalists have so often seemed to define themselves through opposition to their neighbours that Karl Deutsch, a Czech political scientist, defined the nation as 'a group of people united by a mistaken view about the past and a hatred of their neighbours'.[17]

This perspective forces us to question the viability of a truly global nation which has no neighbours to hate. Can we unite without such an external threat? As I researched for this book, this was the challenge most often raised against the viability of my premise. Doesn't every nation need a bogeyman, an 'other'?

Of course, even without neighbours, humanity still has plenty of dangers to worry about. Through the Global Goals, the world's governments have already agreed on what they are. Ten of the seventeen goals describe what we are *for* – broadly, supporting the most vulnerable people to live decent lives. Of the remaining seven, one concerns preventing war and the other six cover different aspects of preserving the environment and its ecosystems. Failure to do either of these really does present an existential threat to humanity. Our task is to rethink our enemies as those dangers, rather than any broadly defined groups of people. That may sound like an impossible conceptual leap, but it is also a necessary one. In the face of necessity, humankind has often been able to adapt in such a way.

In the world today, the destructive power of new weapons means that out-and-out war between major powers is no longer an option in order to preserve life as we know it. The nation-state system was designed for a world where war was certainly destructive but also quite frequently a profitable exercise for at least one of the parties. At stake were the lives of individual citizens and the potential to win, or lose, stretches of territory. But life itself would not be radically altered once the war was over. Today, a conflict between great powers could permanently destroy those major cities which represent the lion's share of the global economy, rendering large parts of the earth uninhabitable, and have knock-on effects on climate that are hard to predict.[18]

This destructive potential has already been demonstrated by events such as the Chernobyl nuclear-reactor explosion in 1986, which has rendered great expanses of land in Eastern Europe uninhabitable to the present day,[19] or the 2003 Iraq War, during which American troops used depleted uranium in their tank shells, allegedly leading to massive increases in birth defects and cancer which Iraqis will have to live with for decades to come.[20] Horrific as they are, these events pale into insignificance when compared to an all-out war between great powers.

This realization, in the aftermath of two world wars, spurred the creation of the global system we live under today, and at its core the United Nations – a body specifically designed to prevent the recurrence of war between major powers. But those institutions on their own are not enough. To complete the job, we need to build the kind of social solidarity without which institutions cannot thrive.

Some might argue that the current system is quite capable of mitigating the threat of global conflagration. Mutually assured destruction, they would argue, is enough of a threat to concentrate minds. By this logic, we do not need a shared identity, or a stronger global system, to avoid a disaster that would be in no one's best interests.

This point of view is highly complacent. Since 1945, we have been living through a period during which a world war with tens of millions of victims – culminating in the use of nuclear weapons on urban civilian populations – was in living memory. That period is coming to an end, as the last remaining Second World War veterans pass away. Those who lived through the war have already ceased to occupy positions of power. In another sixty years, there will be almost no one who has been alive long enough even to hear about the last world war directly from someone who lived through it. To expect that the logic of mutually assured destruction will continue to operate indefinitely is to underestimate the unique psychology of the post-war period.

As American hegemony is gradually but inevitably eroding, a far more challenging period is set to come. The current realignment of geopolitics is producing significant risk of major-power conflict in the coming decades. Such a conflict could easily be so damaging as to relegate the issue of Islamist terrorism to a historical footnote by comparison.

The most frequently cited concern is the rise of China, which has raised the spectre of a 'Thucydides trap', the supposedly inevitable war between an incumbent great power and its newly emerging rival first identified by the Greek historian in his description of Sparta's war with Athens in the fifth century.

However, there is another threat to the US-led order which has been far less noticed but is no less important – the threat from within. The United States may be spending unprecedented amounts on defence, but already it is baulking at the economic burden. It is asking its allies to shoulder an increasing share of the cost, and duties, of defending the geo-strategic status quo. The European Union is being forced to spend more. The Arab Gulf countries, already big military spenders, are being asked to take on a wider military role in confronting America's enemies in the Middle East. Japan is building up its military – officially known as a 'self-defence force' – and its prime minister is seeking to amend its pacifist constitution, allowing it to project far more military might.

The inevitable consequence of an alliance backed less exclusively by American arms is an alliance that the US has less power to control, as can already be seen in the Saudi-led war in Yemen and the EU's refusal to join the US in withdrawing from the Iranian nuclear deal. When we think about the coming multipolar world, then, we need to consider not only the rise of China, India, Russia and other emerging economies but also the potential for America's previously watertight alliance to disaggregate into more egalitarian and some-times conflictual relationships.

We have also been living through a period where nuclear-weapon technology has been relatively new and therefore relatively hard to obtain. That has limited its spread and therefore limited the number of potential configurations for nuclear showdowns. But that picture is rapidly changing, with an increasing number of countries, and therefore potential conflicts, being nuclearized. The existing world system has proven so far able to restrain nuclear weapons' repeated use but has been completely incapable of preventing their spread.

The long period that has passed since the last major power conflict and the fact that we now live in a time of rapidly developing technology are gradually increasing the uncertainty for each power as to who would win, should a conflict take place. According to game theory, violent conflict can normally only be justified by information imbalance. If we knew from the start who the victor would be, we would be inclined to go straight to the peace treaty without undergoing losses on either side. The United States clearly demonstrated itself to have the most powerful military in the world in 1945. Few doubt that it retains the most advanced capabilities. But as time goes by without a head-to-head war between the great powers, rapidly advancing countries like China may begin to question that claim. A turning point could certainly be reached if any country believed they had the technological ability to shut down the nuclear weapons of their enemies. This belief – however true it turned out to be – would create a powerful logic for launching a war and even a first nuclear strike.

Perhaps more likely than a great power conflict is ethnic cleansing on a global scale. A survey of thirty-eight countries in 2017 found that the international terrorist group Islamic State was seen as the number-one threat globally, beating climate change, cyberattacks, the rise of China or US power and influence. The world is already prepared to unite to crush Islamic State and similar groups, with even hostile powers like Russia and the United States tripping over each other to eliminate them in Syria. But there is a dangerously slippery slope from this understandable targeting of terrorist groups and generalized hatred of all Muslims.

The war on terror has already been used on many occasions as a cover to suppress Muslim minorities.[21] Now, a set of explicitly anti-Muslim parties and groups have sprung up and won popular support, especially in Europe and in the United States. The *Guardian* has shown how this anti-Muslim movement is increasingly globally co-ordinated.[22] In 2012, George Morgan, an Australian academic, called Islamophobia 'the world's first global moral panic'; it had turned Muslims into a 'transnational folk devil'.[23] In the coming years, there is a significant risk that this global panic turns into a global pogrom.

While tensions between the US and China threaten a major-power conflagration from which no side would emerge unscathed, punishing Muslims is worryingly easy to achieve. The only nuclear-armed Muslim-majority state is Pakistan, a tiny economy with many institutional weaknesses and rampant poverty. Pakistan would be unlikely to present itself as an immovable object in the face of a coordinated global attack on Muslims.

This is not a prediction that Islamophobia will turn into genocide. It is merely a warning that, as the global community coalesces, we must be vigilant. Such atrocities are characteristic of how national communities have formed in the past. We need to make sure the global nation is different.

This may sound like wishful thinking. You could make the argument that we have always turned on our neighbours, so we will always continue to do so, for such is the unchanging nature of mankind. But this view fails to take into account the many ways that we have shaped and channelled human nature in the past through the invention of cultural traditions. We may not have succeeded in changing the underlying instincts bequeathed to us by evolution but we have very often defanged them.

Two institutions that were born in the age of nationalism show clearly how we have tamed our baser instincts: team sport and multi-party electoral politics.[24] Team sport channels the natural desire for groups of humans to challenge, fight and dominate each other, transforming it into a safe and pleasant pastime. The townspeople of Manchester can march into Liverpool – or vice versa – inflict a crushing defeat on their long-standing opponents and march home victoriously. Throughout the exercise, both sides exhibit a furious passion for their local identity. But it happens peacefully within a national community where, at the end of the day, we are all afforded the same rights.

Meanwhile, multiparty electoral politics regulates humans' desire to overthrow the dominant leader in the group. Throughout much of history, the idea that challengers with new ideas and a different support base could come to prominence and ultimately dethrone the ruler of a community in a peaceful and fair process where no one was killed or imprisoned would have seemed impossible. Political transitions seemed necessarily to involve violence because that is how it had always been done. Indeed, there are still many places where that tradition seems depressingly hard to budge.

Sport and democratic politics demonstrate that many different groups, each with strong identities and the desire for solidarity against an 'other', can coexist within the embrace of a far broader nationalist feeling. These institutions can form the basis for the continuance of deeply held local identities within a global nation. But how to build that broader, global identity without the helpful uniting force of an external, human enemy? That will require the invention of a new set of conventions. We cannot play football, or compete in elections, against a rival that does not exist. So we need to refocus the survival instinct away from the human 'other', uniting instead against the forces that do threaten to destroy us.

It is instructive that protecting the planet takes up fully six of the seventeen Global Goals. While the destructive potential of war provided the impetus to create the global system we live in, rising fears about climate change and mass extinction are the single biggest factors driving the political will for global action today. As with the threat of nuclear war, climate change has a powerful effect on global psychology because it threatens to affect so much of the world's population and may harm the wealthy as well as the poor. While neither threatens to permanently eradicate human life, both could effectively wipe out some of our major cities on every continent.

Sadly, the political will for action is often not found until threats become reality. The United Nations was not formed until after Hiroshima and Nagasaki – as well as Berlin, Manila and many other cities – had been levelled. It may be that the necessity of uniting as humanity in the face of nuclear war and climate change does not focus minds until after one or the other has caused unthinkable chaos. But that grim possibility does not argue for us sitting on our hands. Building a new nation, building new conventions and ways of thinking that channel and refocus human instincts, this is all the work of generations. The time to start is always now.

It seems to me that one of the most productive avenues, acknowledging that we instinctively see other people as our enemies, is to personify the dangers that we face. There is nothing new in that. From Ancient Greek and Roman gods which personified places such as the sea (Poseidon/Neptune) or phenomena such as war (Ares/Mars), to ancient Chinese Tudi Gong, the Mongols' sky-god, or place-based deities from so-called 'animist' religions across Africa and the Americas, such personification has been the norm. Within Hinduism, it still happens. According to Pankaj Mishra, there is now a goddess of AIDS in some Hindu communities (she both causes and cures the disease.)[25]

Elsewhere, a new cultural form has allowed us to imagine not only the personification of a non-human enemy but also the uniting of all humanity to face that threat. Science fiction and, in particular, the trope of alien attack, having been almost completely absent from literature before the twentieth century, has become a peculiar passion in the cultural lives of millions of people. How to explain this phenomenon? Certainly, it is in part a cultural reaction to space exploration, which, in the mid-twentieth century, pushed back the boundaries of human knowledge, and mobility. No doubt it is also a response to the real possibility, sharpened by modern scientific discovery, that there is life outside our planet after all. But mostly I would argue that our relatively recent fascination with films, books and all manner of other portrayals of extraterrestrial enemies is driven by the new-found strength of our identity as humans and the instinctive desire to defend that group against a tangible, external 'other'.

In religion, then, as well as in science fiction, we have the traditions on which to build powerful narratives of what we are against. To reinvent these traditions for the twenty-first century, we should again go back to the classroom. Children respond particularly well to the personification of abstractions. I have seen that for myself in the school I helped create in North London. There, children learn from the age of four about our values – scholarship, teamwork, responsibility, and so on. Each value is represented as a cartoon character, which the children imagine as a person who embodies that value. It is amazing to see how much the pupils relate to the values when personified. From the youngest ages, they can explain which is their favourite one, and why.

A personification of climate change may not change our behaviour overnight – although the recent tradition of giving human names to storms is an example of exactly that. Meteorologists discovered that if storms have specific names, it is easier to rally public interest in avoiding the dangers they present.[26] But if generations of children are brought up with a clear and consistent personification of global threats, from war to climate change, it would stick with them for life. In this way, over a period of generations, it would be possible to reimagine our instinctive hostility to 'the other', forming a global nation in the face of real, but not human, threats.

Principle 3: Defend the nation-state

*The fight now is between those who believe the nation
state is an obstacle to be thrown out and those who believe
it's a jewel to be polished.*

– Steve Bannon, June 2018

Globalists, we are told, are trying to weaken and ultimately destroy
the system of nation-states that has operated since the Peace of Westphalia in 1648.[1] For hundreds of millions of people in rich countries,
their citizenship is by far the most valuable asset they own. It is
unsurprising that this view of globalism has turned many of them
against it.

In fact, few people are calling for such an outcome. Far more
often, anti-globalists make this claim in order to present globalists as
a threat.[2] But the claim is so powerful – and so widely believed – that
it must be refuted clearly and definitely. We need to explain precisely
how a global layer of identity, and governance, will in fact protect
nation-states, rather than weaken them. We need to reject the false
dichotomy that is so often presented between strengthening individual countries and strengthening the global system. Far from being an
obstacle, the continuance of the nation-state is absolutely essential
for the peaceful creation of a more united world.

It became fashionable in the 1990s to argue that the nation-state was
in decline. Books such as Walter Wriston's *The Twilight of Sovereignty* (1993), Kenichi Ohmae's *The End of the Nation State* (1995)
and Susan Strange's *The Retreat of the State* (1996) either cooed or

fretted about the impact of globalization and technology on politics and society. This did not remain a purely academic debate. In 1996, Chancellor Kohl of Germany stated that 'the nation-state cannot solve the great problems of the twenty-first century'.[3]

The argument has followed approximately the same lines ever since: states have lost their monopoly on the economy, on identity and even on violence. They are buffeted by increasingly transnational or global forces in the face of which they are powerless to act. Some formerly state-owned functions are being carried out by international bodies such as the World Trade Organization (WTO), the World Bank, the European Union and the United Nations. Others are being carried out by a rampant global capitalism that respects no borders or governments. Worse still, some functions are not being carried out at all, leading to growing inequality and popular dissatisfaction.

While there is some merit to each of these arguments, they do not add up to the demise of the nation-state. For it to be in terminal decline, there must have been some heyday in the past, where its powers were greater. But as historian Aviei Roshwald has shown,[4] it is hard to substantiate this claim for any previous period.

Prior to the First World War, vast swathes of the world were ruled by empires, and where nation-states existed they were much thinner organizations than they are now, by which I mean they had far lower levels of taxation, welfare and mass political participation than in the present day. In the interwar period, many countries ring-fenced their economies and expanded the voting franchise, but empires remained in place and the entire nation-state system stood at the precipice of the collapse that was the Second World War. After 1945, the empires finally dissolved into a proliferation of new nation-states (the number of which doubled between 1950 and 2000). But just as the nation-state became the norm on every continent, those international bodies accused of snatching away their sovereignty were created. Furthermore, the Cold War circumscribed the freedom of movement of many countries, which were pulled into a clientelist relationship with one or other of the superpowers.

Roshwald concludes that it is since the fall of the Berlin Wall (i.e. precisely the period when it became fashionable to claim they were in decline) that nation-states have become most powerful. To a great degree, that is thanks to the global norms and institutions that are held responsible for sucking away their sovereignty. Under the protection of those norms and institutions, smaller states have a chance of going it alone with some degree of autonomy.

The supposed heyday of the nation-state was in fact a time of great vulnerability for most. Of course, there was a small group of countries that acted without many constraints and did not need to share sovereignty with outside bodies. Britain, France, the United States, Russia and for a brief period Italy, Germany and Japan all felt strong enough to project power abroad and submitted themselves to no international oversight or meddling. To citizens of those countries, the present day may seem to have constrained the power of the nation-state, because their country must now submit, at least in word if not in deed, to an international system. But the truth is that the very freedom of action they enjoyed in the past – the freedom to invade, to enforce regime change and to influence policy of other countries – is the chief reason that, for most of the world, the independent nation-state was far from being fully realized at that time. Conversely, the (very limited) constraints that the global system has put on the most powerful countries has provided a boost to the sovereignty of most others.

If the nation-state never really had the heyday which many people imagine, much of the news of its demise is exaggerated. In international affairs, the bullies are still bullies, as demonstrated by military intervention in Iraq in 2003, Ukraine in 2015 and other conflicts which have gone ahead without the United Nations' blessing. Meanwhile, at home, the state is still the biggest show in town. In most rich countries, government expenditure accounts for somewhere between a third and a half of the entire national economy. Not only is the state still huge in rich countries; in several, the last two decades have actually seen the proportion of the economy controlled by the state rise significantly – growing since 1995 from 54 per cent to more than 56 per cent in France, and from 39 per cent to 41 per cent in the UK. In Japan government expenditure has grown from 36 per cent to 39 per cent of GDP since 2005.[5]

In less wealthy countries, governments control a somewhat smaller proportion of the economy, but this, too, has risen in the last two decades.[6] Given how fast many of those economies, such as China, India, Turkey and Indonesia, have grown in the last twenty-five years, these increases often represent a huge expansion of government spending power.

Governments, then, more than ever dwarf all other players in most national economies. And despite globalization, it still does make sense to talk about 'national economies'. The reason citizenship of a rich country is still so valuable is that labour markets are still isolated enough – despite immigration and off-shoring – to offer a wage premium to local residents, and governments are able to invest more in raising the productivity of workers through education and infrastructure. No wonder, then, that the nation-state remains important to individual citizens. Millions of migrants risk their lives every year to change which one they belong to.

For the majority who stay at home, the nation-state also looms large. The ISSP survey of 45,000 people which gave us the striking results about global citizenship in Chapter 2, also asks people how they feel about the nation-state in which they live. Their responses reveal that the nation-state has lost none of its pull on the heart-strings. Globally, less than 3 per cent of people say that they are 'not close at all' to their country, while fully 87 per cent say they are 'close' or 'very close'. These proportions have not changed significantly since the question was first asked. If the nation-state collapsed during that time, people do not seem to have noticed.

One of the main reasons for the disconnect between this reality and the narrative of the nation-state's decline is a confusion between true loss of power and mere delegation of activity. One thing that is true of countries all over the world is that, since the 1980s, they have handed the management of many activities previously carried out by employees of the state to other actors, either in the private sector or international bodies. Industries, from train services to steel production to power generation, which in many countries had been nationalized, were handed back to private operators. Even in areas where the government continued to pay for services, they were sometimes contracted out, whether in health care, education or social services. Where an economic benefit was seen to be possible through closer harmonization, international organizations – whether trade arbitration bodies or, in Europe, the expanding European Union – were given the right to manage processes.

All this delegation of activity has created a concern that states have lost sovereignty. How can democratically elected governments implement the will of their electorates, if they have ceded control over so many of the most important functions? The answer is that governments can take back control at any time.

Recent events have demonstrated where real power lies. Britain's membership of the European Union, the United States' membership of NAFTA, China's acceptance of the Bretton Woods institutions (the World Bank and the International Monetary Fund): all these, and other ways in which nation-states have seemed to bind themselves, have shown themselves to be no more than voluntary relationships which will last only so long as decision-makers in each country are convinced of their positive overall value. While many have argued furiously against Brexit, renegotiation of NAFTA or China's creation of a new set of international financial institutions, it is instructive that no one has ever questioned that the nation-states in question have the right to take that course of action, should they choose. The only argument against is that it may not be a good idea.

The truth is that almost no real sovereignty has been irretrievably ceded upwards to international bodies. They have merely been seen as sometimes helpful managers of international processes. The same applies to delegation down to the private sector. The only obstacles for a country to renationalize industries, or take private contracts back in-house, are the expense involved and questions over whether such moves would serve any good purpose. Should the public and decision-makers be convinced that it is worthwhile, any government could take back control in an instant.

Despite their increased delegation of activities, nation-states remain by far the most powerful organizing unit of humanity because they have retained their popular legitimacy. We have already seen that a vast, and stable, majority of people feel close to their country. To this it can be added that consistently between 87 per cent and 88 per cent of people over the last three decades say they think it is 'important to respect their country's political institutions and laws'. What's more, nearly 40 per cent in 2013 said that they think people should 'support their country, even when it is in the wrong', and this number has risen significantly since 1995, when only 33 per cent agreed.[7]

It is worth pausing to note how strong an endorsement of the nation-state that last finding represents. To agree that people should support 'their country', even it is in the wrong, implies that they see 'their country' as being capable of having a single position, or taking a specific decision. That is not possible if they see their country as a collection of millions of individuals and various plots of land. It only makes sense if the country's government is an embodiment of the country as a whole – its land, its people and its will. That is the premise of the nation-state. The survey data suggests that a large and growing number of people not only buy into this premise, they are so loyal to the institution of the nation-state that they will follow where it leads, right or wrong.

Of course, not all states are as strong as others. But weak states are nothing new. And even the weakest have proven surprisingly resilient. Sub-state and non-state actors in recent years have mostly proven little match for state power. There has never been a time where states had a complete monopoly on violence in every place on earth, and it is true that there continue to be examples of weak states which are unable to fully dominate violent competitors. This is particularly the case in the present period in the Middle East and parts of Africa. In Lebanon, Hizbollah is a stronger military force than the Lebanese Army. In the Democratic Republic of Congo, the government's powers of enforcement are limited beyond certain strategic locations where their forces are concentrated. But even in the weakest states, what rebels almost always most want is to take over the nation-state rather than to dissolve it.

While we are all rightly concerned about the places where states are collapsing, it is easy to forget that there are at least as many examples of states which have strengthened in recent years. Iraq's and Syria's states looked on the verge of complete collapse in 2014. Now, they have reasserted a great degree of control, albeit at a terrible cost. Colombia is a transformed country in the last decade, as the balance of power has shifted decisively in favour of the government. Decades-long civil wars in Angola, Mozambique and Ethiopia are now distant memories. In India and Nepal long-running Maoist insurgencies have faded.

Overall, the number of attempted *coups d'état* has crashed from a high of nearly fifteen per year in the mid-1950s to less than five per year since 2000.[8] Meanwhile, the number of people killed each year in civil wars has tragically spiked in recent years due to the awful conflicts in Syria and Yemen, but is not above historical averages and is still less than half of the nearly 100,000 people per year who were killed in civil wars in the mid-1980s. The lowest number of civil-war deaths since the Second World War was recorded as recently as 2005.[9]

So it is wrong to characterize our time as one of unprecedented global chaos and state implosion. One of the reasons that many people have developed this view is the unprecedented number of refugees and displaced people worldwide. The total number has now passed 65 million, far more than even at the end of the Second World War. This is indeed a serious cause for concern and represents one of the gravest challenges our world faces. But this large number of displaced people is not easily explained by the nation-state system being weaker than ever. It can more readily be explained by three very different factors: people even in relatively poor countries are more mobile than ever before; improved care for refugees has made the difficult decision to flee violence slightly less risky; and countries affected by instability tend to have extremely high population growth. The large number, and increased mobility, of people suffering from violence and instability has made the problem of weak states seem more pressing, especially to countries receiving refugees. But the problem itself is not new.

The feeling that the nation-state is in decline is a thoroughly European and North American phenomenon and is tightly linked to the perception of decline in those regions. It is not a feeling shared by those in states like Ethiopia and the Philippines where rapid economic growth has lifted tens of millions of people out of poverty and economic migrants are beginning to return home to set up businesses and contribute to their country's development. It is also not shared by those in states like China and Russia whose governments have lost none of their tight control over information and public action, despite the dawn of the internet age.

If nation-states are as powerful now as they have ever been, what does that mean for the global order? My contention is that there is far less tension between the nation-state and globalism than is often claimed. Globalists should defend and strengthen the nation-state for a number of reasons: because the vast majority of people are attached to their nation-states; because identities are built in layers, so strengthening one layer does not require the weakening of another; and because a stronger global system can be a far better protection for the nation-states than the dog-eat-dog world favoured by anti-globalists.

A global nation can be built only through broad consensus. It probably cannot – and certainly should not – be imposed from above. The reason that it is worthwhile to build a nation for humanity is that nationalism has shown itself to be such a powerful unifying force. To recognize this is to accept that existing national identities are deeply held and will not be easily renounced.

Happily, they need not be. Following Karl Marx, early communists called for an end to all national identities. They saw the inevitable victory of an undifferentiated global proletariat against the religions, nations and other group identities that had been created to divide and rule them. But that particular globalist vision did not get very far. By the 1930s, communists had 'reclaimed the badge of nationalism'.[10] Other attempts to unify broad groups of people have been more successful, precisely because they have not attempted to stamp out all differences.

The examples of Europe, the United States and India are instructive. In Europe, the creation of nation-states hundreds of years ago has still not diminished the regional identities within them. A 2014 survey of European identity found that in almost every one of the fourteen sub-national regions surveyed, more people feel 'very close' to their local region, closer than to their nation-state. Regional identity trumps national identity in some places by huge margins, not only where there are independence movements, such as in Scotland and Catalonia, but also in places with no strong urge to secede, like Brittany in France and Thuringia in Germany. In France in particular, stronger regional identities did not go alongside any rejection of France as a whole. Most people are very comfortable with the different layers of their identity. When asked whether their identity is primarily regional or primarily national, by far the most common answer was that it is 'equally split' between the two.[11]

More recently, Europeans have been experimenting with the creation of an even larger political system, and identity, on top of its nation-states. It is still far from clear how successful European integration will be over the long term. It certainly shows that such a feat cannot be achieved overnight. But the reason European integration is so tortuous and unpredictable is precisely because it is being advanced only with the consensus of the nation-states that form its constituent parts. They are willing participants because they see integration as protecting and advancing their interests, not because they want to make themselves redundant. However integrated Europe becomes, there will always remain distinct political traditions, and identities, separating Germans from Italians and Poles from Greeks.

Meanwhile, the United States and India both provide examples of how highly diverse, continent-sized nations can be built. Neither has a spotless record. Both countries in their founding exemplify how nation-building can go wrong. The United States was founded on claims of equal citizenship, freedom and democracy, but its early leaders interpreted this as applying only to Europeans, as their treatment of their Native American and African neighbours shows. In the case of India, as nationalists argued for independence from Britain, they were unable to convince the people living in Muslim-majority provinces that their best interests lay in a united country. The result was partition, which brought ethnic cleansing on both sides, with the death of perhaps 1 million people. Nor have the problems gone away. In both countries, intercommunal tensions have increased recently in connection with the rise to power of divisive populists who seem content to represent only one ethnic group.

However, both India and the United States show how diverse political traditions and identities can be enshrined while building a national bond that encompasses them all. In the United States, each state entered the union willingly as a sovereign entity, which, as part of the union, shares its sovereignty with the federal government. Two hundred and fifty years later, US states continue to command deep feelings of attachment and loyalty, to house their own democratic representation and to perform important governmental functions.

Much like the European Union, the United States evolved over time. In its early years, the US was no more a united nation than the

EU is today. The first version of the federation, enshrined in the Articles of Confederation, created a US Congress where each state voted as a block, rather than lawmakers from congressional districts operating independently of their states. Any decision required the approval of nine out of thirteen states and major changes of policy required unanimity. Furthermore, there was no fiscal or monetary union across the states, a situation which persisted for several decades. The word 'nation' is used only once in the Declaration of Independence, and there it refers to Great Britain. It is used only once in the Articles of Confederation, and there it refers to a group of Native Americans. It is used twice in the US Constitution, again referring only to other countries. However, by the end of the nineteenth century, things had advanced greatly. Along with stronger federal institutions, there was a greater sense of nationhood. The pledge of allegiance, first drafted in 1892, was proud to declare that the United States was 'one nation, indivisible'.[12]

Uniting India was even more ambitious. As recently as 1860, the entire global human population was equal to the 1.3 billion currently residing in India.[13] Unlike the United States, the majority of India's population are established communities which have lived in that country for hundreds, if not thousands, of years. They display a huge variety of language, religion and custom. A century ago, a single Indian nation seemed to be an impossible dream. In 1888, Sir John Strachey, a senior British civil servant who had spent most of his life in India, wrote: 'This is the first and most essential thing to learn about India – that there is not, and never was ... any sort of unity, physical, political, social, or religious; no Indian nation, no "people of India" ... It must not be supposed that such bonds of union can in any way lead towards the growth of a single Indian nationality.'[14]

But despite the trauma of partition, the rump of the country has shown itself capable of incorporating its various communities, including Muslims. While the flare-ups of intercommunal violence which have occurred since partition are worrying, no less so now that the Hindu-nationalist Bharatiya Janata Party is in power, it is remarkable how peacefully the communities have lived side by side since the 1950s. This is a country that was founded only seventy years ago, where, historically, Muslims and Hindus on the whole refused to intermarry or even to eat with each other; where the traditional heroes of one religious community were the villains of the other; where partition created hostile Muslim states at the border which could easily lead to Indian Muslims being labelled a 'fifth column'.

Not only that, 70 million Indians belong to marginalized and far less developed tribal groups located in the Himalayan north-east or mountainous central belt. There is a linguistic divide that splits the various, interrelated languages of the Indo-European North from the Dravidian tongues of the South. There are various religious minorities – Buddhists, Parsees, Jains, Christians and Sikhs – besides the 20 per cent who are Muslims. Layered on top of this, vast socio-economic differences, deeply entrenched in culture through the caste system, mean that many of the richest people in the world share a country with hundreds of millions in absolute poverty. And yet the nation did form, cohere and thrive. According to ISSP, two thirds of Indians feel 'very close' to their country.

Again, the Indian national identity has been built by reinforcing and protecting the identities of each community rather than trying to erase them. This can be seen in the evolution of the state boundaries in India, which have been radically redrawn since independence to reflect the communities to which Indians feel they belong. India inherited the British Empire's division of its territories, which followed the historical accidents of conquest and treaties. Their realignment bears much in common with the movements for national self-determination in Central and Eastern Europe which redrew the map of that region after 1990.

If the redrawing of the map of nation-states over the last hundred years is associated with 'national self-determination' (a term US President Woodrow Wilson first popularized as his preferred principle for shaping a post-imperial world), then India's redrawing of state boundaries has been the result of sub-national self-determination. To give one of several examples, in 1956, after long and at times explosive campaigning, including the death through self-starvation of popular Telugu leader Potti Sreeramulu, the central government agreed to create the new state of Andhra Pradesh as a separate state for speakers of the Telugu language. This involved splitting off and combining the Telugu-speaking areas of the former Madras and Hyderabad states.

Such reorganization in response to popular demands has happened repeatedly since the 1950s and continues to this day.

The persistence of sub-national self-determination movements in India forces us to reconsider the true significance of nationalist movements today. It is an article of faith among watchers of international politics that the persistence and rise of nationalist movements are always by their nature anti-globalist and represent a fracturing of international cooperation. India's recent history suggests that this need not be the case – demands for more local autonomy and independence are perfectly consistent with the development of a common identity which transcends local differences.

The above examples are instructive, but they do not provide a model for a global nation. Even such large and diverse places as the European Union, the United States and India are on a different scale of complexity than the world today. There is no appetite, or need, to create a global federal government such as exists in the US or India. My suggestions for the reforms we do need in the global political system are outlined in Chapter 8, where I argue that the system needs to be bolstered in just four ways: enforcing tax coordination, enforcing the implementation of climate-change commitments, assessing and distributing refugees for resettlement (all with the threat of economic sanctions) and creating a more consensus-based decision-making process for the rare cases where the use of force is necessary. All of these changes are designed to strengthen nation-states by protecting them from rogue actors.

These changes will not come overnight. In the meantime, globalists must be careful not to undermine the most precious institution that many nation-states contain – democracy. The outsized influence elites wield means that when most of the elite disagree on important issues with the majority of the people, democracy, where it exists, is endangered. An extreme example is Thailand, where, during the premiership of Thaksin Shinawatra from 2001 to 2006, a large section of the military, economic and political elite decided that his electorally popular programme was unacceptable. This elite backlash against the democratic will led to multiple military coups and eventually to what looks at the time of writing to be a long-term cancellation of proper democratic process. Egypt's short-lived democratic experiment suffered the same fate in 2013 when the established classes refused to accept government by the Muslim Brotherhood.

In more established democracies, there is less risk that events would spiral so far out of hand, but the subtle undermining of popular will remains a problem. Globalists tend to worry about the danger to democracy posed by anti-globalist populists, but they can themselves be just as undemocratic. The promulgation of the Lisbon Treaty in the European Union is a good example. The treaty was a successor to the European Constitution, which had been scrapped in 2005 after being rejected by referenda in France and the Netherlands. However, the Lisbon Treaty contained almost identical provisions to those in the rejected Constitution. This time, there was less willingness to consult the population. Only Ireland (which was constitutionally compelled to do so) held a vote, in 2008, and this also yielded a 'no' result. But the Irish referendum was rerun a year later, eventually producing the approval desired by pro-Europeans. The rest of Europe's governments signed off on the treaty without further sanction from their electorates.

None of this implies the end of democracy as such, as it is not a condition of democracy that decisions must be made by referendum. But in the eyes of many people the implementation of a treaty which had – in its essence – been specifically rejected by Dutch, French and Irish voters looked like a conspiracy by the elite to pursue international integration and ignore the popular will. This is no isolated example. It is part of a worrying, generalized global trend towards fewer, weaker democracies over the last decade. In January 2018, the Economist Intelligence Unit's Democracy Index found that 89 out of 167 countries they assessed had a lower overall score for the health of their democracies than in the previous year.[15]

To be clear, I am not calling for any attempt to implant democracy where it does not currently exist. Part of the continued sovereignty of nation-states must include each states' right to determine its own political system. However, it is extremely important that globalists do not undermine democracy where it exists. Not only would that be morally wrong, it is also doomed to failure, as witnessed by the anti-globalist backlash in many countries. Pro-Europeans at the time looked at the passage of the Lisbon Treaty as a great victory, but that victory is fast becoming Pyrrhic as voters in Britain, Italy and elsewhere choose governments promising to remove them from treaties which they increasingly feel they were bullied into. The result has been a long-term loss of trust in the political class in Europe and North America.

Pursuing globalism while protecting the nation-state means that globalists need to be far more attentive supporters of democracy. Where the consensus is against them, they must give ground. The most significant area where they must do so is on immigration, which is the subject of the next chapter.

Principle 4: If you love
mobility, let it go

> *No offspring of southern barbarians will be allowed to remain. Anyone violating this order will be killed, and all relatives punished according to the gravity of the offence.*
> – Shogun Tokugawa Iemitsu, Edict for
> the Seclusion of Japan (1635)[1]

The realization of the global nation is in conflict with one of the powers that nation-states have in recent times held most dear: the power to control who enters, and on what terms. One thing that all nations have in common, whatever their governmental arrangements, is the understanding that co-nationals should be allowed to travel freely within the nation's territory. This is an implication of some of the nation's defining myths: that we all are equal before the law; that we all belong to a single family; that we are bound by bonds of trust. That is why the growth of nationalism encouraged the removal of barriers that restricted internal movement within a country, for example through Russia's abolition of serfdom in the 1860s.[2]

So a truly global nation implies a world of free movement. For much of the period in which nationalism took root, freedom of movement between countries was the norm.[3] But today it is implacably opposed by many of those calling themselves nationalists. Should globalists call for borders to be flung open again? In my view, although universal free movement is a desirable goal and a necessary end point, it should not be implemented or attempted in this generation. Only after significant progress on cultural and economic convergence will the world be ready to benefit from it without overriding costs.

Globalists should support nation-states' democratic right to self-determination – including deciding who can enter the country – even when the results run counter to their longer-term ambitions. While making the case for a world of free movement, globalists should be content to focus on keeping the doors open to students and refugees. Just as maintaining the nation-state does not mean forgoing steps to a greater political unity, so immigration controls will not end the processes that are shaping globalist identity.

Globalists in rich countries tend to be very relaxed about immigration. While perhaps the majority are happy to live in a world with some immigration controls, they are also happy to see their neighbourhood, and their country as a whole, become increasingly diverse. While stopping short of arguing that Europe and the United States should remove all border patrols on their southern peripheries, they oppose the kind of measures, such as tighter border security, or extra-territorial asylum-processing centres, which would be likely to prevent most illegal crossings. Conversely, they support policies such as regularizing undocumented immigrants, unworried about the potential to incentivize an increase in the number of new arrivals. These stances are justified by the fact that they see immigration as broadly positive. They see benefits for the migrants, who should be allowed to pursue happiness wherever they want, and benefits for the destination country, due to the hard work of people who have shown a willingness to make great sacrifices in order to be part of it.

Most globalists in less wealthy countries share this comfort with migration, albeit from a different perspective – a more liberal attitude to immigration stands to benefit them the most. For some, their globalist identity will be inseparable from their personal desire to travel, whether temporarily or permanently. But even if they do not intend to migrate themselves, they are unlikely to be comfortable with a world where most wealth is locked away in countries which they and their fellow citizens may not be allowed to enter.

Some have gone so far as to argue for a world of unrestricted free movement. Typical of this view are Bryan Caplan and Vipul Naik, whose 2014 paper 'A Radical Case for Open Borders' argues that global free movement is economically and morally compelling, calling the current system of controls 'a radical abridgment of free-dom based on an arbitrary distinction, propped up by status quo bias and moral apathy'.[4] Conveniently for such globalists, freedom of movement is both right and practical. Caplan and Naik take their economic analysis from Michael Clemens's 2011 paper 'Economics and Migration: Trillion-dollar Bills on the Sidewalk',[5] in which he claims that the likely boost to global GDP from freedom of move-ment would be in the range of 50 per cent to 150 per cent. This argument was picked up in July 2017 by the *Economist*, which ran an article with the headline: 'A world of free movement would be $78 trillion richer.' These authors acknowledge that there will be winners and losers from migration but assert that the overall gains will be so great that anyone suffering negative impacts can be more than com-pensated for their losses through various forms of redistribution. Put like this, it's certainly an attractive proposition: we will all be freer, and richer, with open borders.

This argument has certainly not convinced everyone. Indeed, the battle to reduce immigration has, more than any other issue, united ethno-nationalists across the rich world. Donald Trump's supporters come from both the left and the right on economics, and on foreign policy contain both hawks and isolationists. But on this they are unanimous: immigration into America should be reduced. Britons who voted to leave the European Union also come from across the political spectrum. Many believe in free trade and are appalled by the trade war that President Trump's administration has waged, but almost all share a desire to 'control borders' (code for reducing the flow). France's Rassemblement National, Italy's La Lega, Germany's AfD, Finland's True Finns, Hungary's Fidesz – they may agree on some things and differ on others, but on no issue are they so aligned as on their opposition to immigration.

What drives this opposition? Like the globalists, they assert that both economics and morality are on their side. They claim that work-ing people have less income, with scarce jobs taken by immigrants prepared to work for less money; that housing is more expensive because of the flood of new people; that health care, schools and roads are filled to breaking point. But more than anything, they are united in the feeling that their country and its culture is changing in ways they do not like and even faces existential threat. David Goodhart, in explaining Brexit and the backlash against immigration, cites the 60 per cent of Britons who in 2011 agreed with the statement: 'Britain has changed in recent times beyond recognition, it sometimes feels like a foreign country and this makes me uncomfortable.'[6] The sentiment is captured powerfully by Douglas Murray, who speaks on behalf of the anti-immigration lobby in *The Strange Death of Europe*. His opening sentence sums up their fears: 'Europe is committing suicide.' In the realm of fiction, the cultural death of Europe has been most famously imagined by Michel Houellebecq, whose 2015 novel *Submission* pictures France transformed into an Islamic state.

Given the concentration of these political forces in rich countries, anti-immigration sentiment can appear to be specific to them. But this is true only because in recent years large-scale immigration has been occurring mainly in rich countries. The US and the UK both now have foreign-born populations of around 15 per cent of the total population. In 1970, the figure was less than 5 per cent in the US and less than 6 per cent in the UK. While in the US this has meant a return to the level it reached at the height of European migration a century ago, in the UK such high levels of immigration are unprecedented. Meanwhile, France and Germany's foreign-born populations have hovered at around 12 per cent over the last decade, with the latter's jumping to 15 per cent in the wake of the recent influx of refugees.[7] Very often, this wave of immigration from poor to rich countries is explained as a natural and even an unstoppable result of globalization, leading those angered by it to take on an anti-globalist stance.

However, the instinct that drives opposition to migration is not limited to ethno-nationalist populists in rich countries. The other large-scale anti-globalist coalition – that of political Islam – is also based on a desire to protect a supposedly threatened cultural identity from outside influences. If there were high levels of immigration into Muslim countries, it is easy to imagine this becoming one of the totem issues for Islamists, in the same way that it is for populists in rich countries. Of course, there is a specific case where this is so. Jewish immigration into Israel/Palestine and the subsequent demographic, cultural and political changes have provided an iconic narrative within Muslim communities of a threat driven by immigration.

The same would be true in many other contexts. For example, India, which has often pushed other countries to relax migration controls, is not comfortable with immigration from Pakistan, with which it maintained effectively closed borders for decades. If there were a mass migration of Pakistanis into India, and a perception that this was driven by globalization, it is highly likely that India's government, and people, would turn decisively towards the anti-globalist position.

So an unwillingness to welcome massive immigration from other countries is far more widespread than it can appear. The very idea of a demographic threat posed by one cultural community to another is antithetical to the idea that we all form a single nation. Clearly, a feeling of global nationhood has not yet developed sufficiently to make everyone comfortable with free movement. But what should come first? The 'chicken' of free movement or the 'egg' of globalist identity? Should people be forced to accept free movement in the hope that soon enough they will get over their fears of it by means of a strengthened globalist identity?

Most globalists yearn for those opposing immigration to put their concerns aside and accept the demographic change it brings as benign and even helpful. From a globalist point of view, talk of threats to a local culture or identity can look like bigotry and even racism: what reason could there be for excluding people when we are all part of a welcoming, global culture? But this hectoring approach is not helpful. Anti-globalist concerns cannot just be wished or lectured away. Instead, we need to understand them.

The moral case for open borders is not as obvious as it first appears. David Miller and Kwame Anthony Appiah have both convincingly argued that a cosmopolitan outlook – broadly welcoming of other people and accepting of some reciprocal duties applying across humanity – does not require that our obligations to all other humans are identical. Even in a cosmopolitan world, we cannot wish to destroy the bonds of family, local community, interest group, and so on. The existence of these groups improves the world for their members and for everyone else. They are part of a well-functioning world.

Such groups depend on the fact that their members have special obligations to each other which they are not expected to fulfil for all of humanity. Local communities watch out for crime against each other's houses, and that keeps crime rates down for everyone. But a local community cannot keep an eye on the houses of every other person in other parts of the world. Parents are expected to house and clothe their children – and it benefits us all that they do – but they cannot be expected to house and clothe every child. To insist that every adult had the same obligations to every child would have the effect of ending the institution of family altogether. In judging whether it was morally wrong for a parent to give special preference to their child, we would need to weigh any 'fairness' gains from equal treatment against the loss of all the benefits the existence of families brings.

The same logic applies to nation-states and immigration. In the absence of an understanding of the real consequences, it cannot be conclusively shown that a system where humans organize themselves into nation-states, which then control entry to their territory, is right or wrong. It is certainly possible to argue that allowing the entry of an individual is an absolute moral obligation when not allowing them to enter would inevitably lead to them suffering grievous harm or death. That is the basis of the internationally recognized (but imperfectly followed) obligation to give asylum to refugees. But beyond that the moral position is murkier.

If it can be shown that allowing unlimited immigration would really provide benefits all round, or at least would provide benefits to many people and harm no one, then it will seem like unreasonable discrimination to prevent people from entering any country. In that case, the claim that the anti-immigration lobby rests on a combination of ignorance and bigotry would be a strong one. But if it can be shown that free movement would be likely to destroy the very fabric of some or all nation-states, reducing or even ending the benefits that the nation-state brings, then this must be strongly weighted against any potential benefits springing from free movement. In such a scenario it would seem reasonable for nation-states to protect their own existence by restricting immigration.

What would be the effect of free movement on the nation-state? To start with, it is universally acknowledged that levels of migration from poorer countries to richer countries would be huge. Most advocates of free movement accept the figures produced by Gallup polls of 156 countries which have consistently found over the last decade that between 13 per cent and 14 per cent of the world's population want to permanently emigrate from their current country of residence. That translates into around 700 million people moving overnight.[8]

In their study, Caplan and Naik note that the population of the United States would increase by 60 per cent; that of Australia would more than double. Poor countries like Haiti would lose a majority of their citizens. Migrants from the poorest countries who arrived in rich-world cities would be wealthier than they had been in their native countries but would still be very poor compared to the average in their new homes. Caplan and Naik describe the likely social effects as follows:

> The shift to labor-intensive occupations will make developed countries look more primitive. Shantytowns may emerge. Some natives will react by helping migrants learn the language, find jobs, and adjust to their new societies. Others will resent new arrivals and pine for the good old days when low-skilled immigration was but a trickle. Before long, however, most natives will, like the Third World middle class, simply learn to tolerate the sight of poverty and inequality.[9]

To many New Yorkers or Sydneysiders, this image might be sufficiently apocalyptic to settle the case against free movement. But if it is an accurate view of the future, it has much to recommend it. If the world's GDP is set to double and all rich countries have to worry about it is the ugly sight of poverty and a little nostalgia, then surely the huge economic benefits can be used to compensate for these losses.

Paul Collier, in *Exodus*, his thoughtful analysis of the likely impacts of increased immigration, offers a more concerning perspective. Rather than accepting that demand for immigration is a fixed figure based on survey results, he argues that the demand for migration is a dynamic quantity, driven above all by the wage gap between the two countries and the size of the sender country's existing diaspora in the receiver country. Collier argues that these forces will generally combine to produce an exponentially expanding demand for immigration to rich countries, as rising immigration produces larger diasporas that are slower to assimilate, driving ever higher levels of migration and ever larger diasporas.

By this logic, the 14 per cent of the world who now want to relocate is just the starting point. Rather than merely rising by 60 per cent as a one-off effect of free movement, the United States population would keep rising inexorably until a radically different dynamic came into play. That new dynamic might be panic-driven immigration controls. Or it could be the breakdown of the state and society.

The economic models that predict massive gains from immigration assume that politics and economics continue to function as normal as each new immigrant arrives. By far the biggest impact of immigration from poor to rich countries is a very large increase in earnings for the immigrant. These gains are far greater than any potential economic losses suffered by others. At least in theory, then, they could be redistributed to ensure that everyone wins.[10] But the total number of people living outside their country of birth is just 220 million worldwide, and immigrants remain by far the minority in almost every country. What if 700 million people were to move overnight or, following Collier, if immigration were to spiral exponentially? Is it reasonable to assume that this number of immigrants would merely add productive workers to an unchanged political and economic system? The honest answer is we just don't know. But a number of studies into the social impact of migration shows that the economic gain to migrants is not the only thing worth considering.

Groundbreaking research by Robert Putnam, himself a supporter of immigration and diversity, has uncovered the social costs of migration.[11] Putnam demonstrated that in communities across the United States, the higher the number of immigrants, the lower the levels of 'social capital', which he defined as 'social networks and the associated norms of reciprocity and trustworthiness'. Americans living in high-immigration communities trust other people less, including even those from their own ethnicity. They report less confidence in local government, local leaders and local news reports. They believe they have less ability to change things and are less likely to register to vote. They have lower expectations of cooperation, donate less time and money to charity and have fewer friends and confidants. Finally, they are less happy, have a lower quality of life and spend more time watching the television.

Could it really be that immigration alone was producing all these effects? It seems so. Putnam's huge sample size across widely different communities in the US allowed him to control for almost every conceivable variable, such as wealth or income inequality, which might have been argued to be the real driver of reduced social capital. But whichever regressions he and his team ran, the result was unchanged. Immigration was making the entire community less happy and connected.

Putnam himself claims that the negative effects he found will reduce over time and gives examples of how diversity can be redefined in order to mitigate these effects. White Americans, for example, now see themselves as a single ethnicity, whereas in the past white Catholics would have seen white Protestants as a culturally different group and therefore a potential source of socially harmful diversity in their neighbourhood. In the same way, the US Army has overcome a historical lack of trust between white and African-American soldiers by building a successful common identity over the last fifty years.

But if a successful group identity is not created, the effects Putnam noticed are likely to linger indefinitely. Strikingly, he found that the negative effects of diversity were still prominent, albeit less pronounced, when involving only white Americans and African-Americans – neither of which are recent immigrant groups. The history of white Americans and African-Americans has of course been very troubled, so it cannot be generalized to all racial or cultural diversity. But it certainly offers an example of how the social impact of diversity can last even hundreds of years after different groups have settled in a country. Given the fraught relationship between Muslims and Christians in Europe, might not those communities also maintain a view of each other over the coming centuries that ossified a perception of 'difference', leading to continued social costs?

Putnam's findings, which have been supported by many other studies across the world in many different social settings, provide two potential objections to the globalist narrative on free movement. First, he found that the negative social effects of migration were offset by increased education and higher incomes. Richer, better educated people may have a cushion of superior social capital which allows them to experience the more fragmented life of a diverse community without tipping into isolation and despair. So it may not be that richer, more educated globalists simply 'get it' and need to explain the benefits of immigration to their fellow citizens. It may be that many people who are against immigration are just living a different social reality, with costs that are invisible to others.

Second, the worrying breakdown in social capital that Putnam observed begs the question: what would be the result if this continued indefinitely? Immigration brings benefits only because the immigrant is moving to a country with successful institutions, which themselves rely on a functioning, trust-based society.

It is impossible to say what unlimited movement of people would do to the level of trust in society. Perhaps there is a limit to the loss of social capital that Putnam observed; that is, after a certain level of diversity, any additional diversity has no further effect. That is perhaps the implication of the pattern of voting in Britain's EU referendum, where the strongest reaction against immigration (measured by the proportion of people voting to leave the EU) was in communities where the proportion of immigrants had risen swiftly but remained at moderately low levels, while areas with very high levels of immigration seemed less opposed.

It may be that societies, despite being put under strain by the social costs of diversity, will maintain diversity's most important strengths and gain new perspectives that are of value. It is possible that competition between different 'ways of doing things', as immigrants bring their expectations and behaviours into an established culture, creates improvements on the existing system. Research in the workplace has revealed that teams with more cultural diversity are more creative than homogeneous teams.[12]

All this suggests the possibility of a hopeful long-term outcome from a world of free movement, where the contact of cultures ends up producing common ground that is an improvement for everyone. It is a nice idea, and it may be true. But I have no hard evidence to demonstrate that it is the inevitable outcome. All I have is a set of hunches based on my reading of world history, which at best imperfectly models the forces that free movement would unleash in the contemporary world.

One does not have to go far back into history to find waves of immigration which redrew the political map to the disadvantage of the native population. European migration to the Americas and Australasia is perhaps the most notable example, although there are many others. Even if the native social norms and institutions in rich countries were maintained, because immigrants choose to adopt them, there is a risk that diasporas will cluster so much in specific regions that soon they would be able to change not only the policies and leadership, but even the political identity, of their new home.

What if so many Cubans poured into Florida that they formed a majority of voters, who then moved for the secession of Florida from the United States, creating a separate nation-state called New Cuba? Is that really so difficult to imagine? After all, Texas became part of the United States in the same way. Previously a sparsely inhabited part of Mexico, from 1822 it welcomed immigrants from the United States, hoping to create a settled agricultural community that could act as a bulwark against raids by the native Comanche tribes. But the plan worked too well. By 1834, the new immigrants formed almost 80 per cent of Texas's population. The next year, they began to violently reject the Mexican government, and by 1836 they had achieved independence. Nine years later the independent state of Texas joined the Union as the twenty-eighth state. Not only had this great chunk of Mexico's territory broken away and changed its political orientation, but the social norms and institutions changed too. Slavery had been illegal in Texas when it was part of Mexico, but it now joined the union as a slave state.

If all that seems far off, then the current threat of terrorism to urban centres across the world provides ample grounds for the anti-immigrant lobby to claim that uncontrolled immigration has the potential to allow people determined to destroy the nation-state to enter it. Clearly, there exist terrorist groups who would dearly love to destroy many nation-states and the societies on which they rest. I am convinced, like many others, that they will never succeed, and that the issue of terrorism can be most effectively dealt with at source by a combination of improved international cooperation, smarter military interventions and economic growth. But that is merely an aspiration. Terrorism is a certain fact, which brutally and randomly snatches away the lives of innocent people. It is unreasonable to expect that it will not turn the attitudes of many citizens against immigration, especially from the places where terrorist organizations are based.

Over the long term, it is impossible to predict what the political results of free movement in the twenty-first century would be, but it is safe to say that they could be significant. Caplan and Naik propose what they call 'key-hole solutions' for such risks: if you are worried about their political impact, do not let immigrants vote. But this is more like a sledgehammer than key-hole surgery. It is morally un-attractive for a state to contain a territory where the majority of people are unable to vote. One could argue that, in doing so, the country would have already sacrificed a great part of its culture. The sledge-hammer might also be ineffective. It would certainly not remove the risk of terrorism, and it might not stop diasporas from eventually taking over. Mexico tried its best to prevent Texas from seceding. But once a population forms a majority in a territory, it is not always straightforward to remove them.

I do not wish to suggest that countries with high levels of immigration are doomed. On the contrary, my personal political stance is towards tolerance for immigration. I have merely tried to demonstrate that those who support controls on immigration have a reasonable arg-ument. The costs they perceive are intangible and elusive: lower levels of trust, sociability and happiness; concerns about the long-term social and political fracturing of the country. These costs are difficult to measure, but that does not mean they are not real.

However, across Europe and the United States, mainstream politi-cal parties have until recently been united in rejecting public demands to reduce immigration, leaving them to be championed by the far right. The message has time and again been given by mainstream parties: if you support policies that are likely to significantly cut immigration, you belong to an extremist fringe and your views are not acceptable. It is unsurprising, then, that frustration has turned to anger and, since 2016, this anger has been channelled into electoral success for the anti-immigrant lobby.

How should responsible globalists respond? Sadly, a common response has been to join Frank Underwood in the TV show *House of Cards* in sighing that 'Democracy is so overrated.'[13] Those in favour of immigration often focus on what they claim is a hard fact: the economic impact, which, although it is difficult to distribute fairly, remains large and positive. Looking only at the economics, they claim that people who are against immigration are simply 'wrong' to oppose it. According to this view, since the public misunderstands the issue, political parties should 'show leadership' and ignore them. Much like the interest rates, which are in many countries set by independent central banks, or the medicine approval authorities that determine the safety of pharmaceutical products without recourse to the electorate, immigration is a complex technical matter which should be decided by 'experts'.

But weighing the economic benefits of immigration against the various, nebulous social costs is not something that lends itself to scientific measurement. It is by definition a matter of subjective judgement. And it is in cases such as these, above all, that democratic decision-making is most appropriate. When an economic benefit has to be weighed against widely dispersed losses in individual people's happiness, an election or referendum through which the public is able to approve or reject the status quo is probably the most scientific way we have to reach a conclusion.

It will come as no surprise that I am an ardent supporter of the European Union. Whatever its imperfections, it offers a shared political and economic system to underpin a common identity that goes beyond the nation-state, albeit one that stops at the European level, rather than extending to all people. I believe the European Union brings economic benefits and, on a social level, I feel close to other Europeans from across its twenty-seven member countries. As a result, I voted for the UK to remain inside the club.

But I have been shocked to observe a near-unanimous position among ardent pro-Europeans, both in the UK and across Europe: that the electorate should not have been given a say. With the vast majority of the political class supportive of European integration, no major party was prepared to put leaving the European Union in their manifesto. So, without a referendum, the only option for supporters of Brexit was to vote for the single-issue and often distasteful UK Independence Party. And yet there was so much strength of feeling against the EU that serious commentators have predicted a UKIP government in the coming years.[14] Most pro-Europeans seem to think that it was sustainable to have no referendum and no mainstream party offering Brexit in their manifesto. That is a deeply undemocratic stance and one which seriously underestimates the long-term consequences of ignoring the popular will.

It comes against a backdrop of sinking support for democracy itself. Research by Yascha Mounk and Roberto Stefan Foa has shown that in Europe support for democracy among people between the ages of sixteen and thirty-four (who are more likely to be pro-immigration liberals) has fallen steadily since the mid-1990s. The number of those saying that democracy is a bad way to run their country has nearly doubled from 6 per cent in 1995 to almost 12 per cent in 2011. The same phenomenon can be seen in the US, where in 2011 almost a quarter of those under thirty-five were against democracy.[15] With our most valuable political institutions under threat, it is irresponsible for globalists to further undermine them, on immigration or on any other issue.

Campaigning to prevent electorates from having a say, or to overturn democratic decisions, is not a good use of the collective energy of globalists. Instead, they should welcome nation-state democracy as the best available system to determine whether the overall societal impacts of immigration remain positive. A vote for reduced immigration is a clear signal that the social costs have begun to outweigh the benefits, meaning that immigration should be slowed. Every time a government promises to do this but refuses to implement the policies that could make it happen, trust in the system falls and the potential for extremist solutions grows.

Surely Robert Putnam was right that the only way to reduce the costs of diversity is to reduce the perception of diversity by building a common identity to which people can attach themselves. That does not mean removing all diversity and difference. Two people can feel they are both Chinese, while one is a Christian Cantonese speaker and the other a Confucian who speaks Mandarin. But it means extending outwards the boundaries of the solidarity that we feel for co-nationals until it reaches all people. At that point, the moral calculation will change – free movement will be accepted as a natural right.

Just as globalists are confident that immigration will not erase the most valuable elements of their culture and will even improve it, they should be confident that the steady march towards a shared global culture and identity will continue, despite the immigration controls. That is because the majority of the work of building global solidarity will not be done by individual people changing their country of residence.

This fact is borne out by the experience of building nations in the past. Italians and Germans through the nineteenth century increasingly came to see themselves as Italians and Germans, rather than citizens of the petty states to which they belonged. But most never left their towns or villages. The same happened in Arab countries and in India in the twentieth century. In the Arab countries a strong nationalist sentiment emerged, despite freedom of movement having never been permitted. Indians were allowed to move across the expanse of their country, but only a small minority did. The conditions for building a globalist identity are therefore already in place.

Applying democratically determined restrictions to immigration will not end this process. In fact, it may speed it up, by removing one of the main sources of anger against the global system. Japan provides an interesting case study in what happens when a rich country accepts only a very small number of immigrants. The result is that it is still outward looking, welcoming to foreign cultural influence and keen to engage with the world. Foreigners are treated with a great deal of respect. Japan is not the kind of narrow-minded dystopia that globalists often fear their country would become if the anti-immigration lobby had its way. And even in Japan, which for hundreds of years was entirely closed to foreigners, the case for more open borders is gradually being won because of the economic and demographic imperatives of a rich, ageing society. The immigration system is in the process of being overhauled, with the intention of allowing far more people to live and work in the country.[16]

While accepting the democratic will on the overall level of immigration, globalists should focus on ensuring that their countries keep two channels of immigration open. Firstly, immigration policies should allow the entry of unlimited numbers of students to access higher education. Foreigners in universities join an already jumbled world of mobile strangers and therefore do not disrupt long-established social structures. They have an unambiguously positive impact on the economy of the country of study, both by paying fees to the university and by spending money in local businesses. Restrictions on employment mean they can be prevented from competing with natives in the labour market. The students benefit as individuals, gaining skills through their course of study as well as international experience and a new international social network of like-minded people. Meanwhile, their country of origin also benefits, because many of those who study abroad, even if they have the option to remain, do return home, bringing their technical expertise and international experience with them.

The circulation of these students is one of the most important engines of globalist identity. The total number of foreign students in the ten most popular destination countries is estimated at 3.7 million.[17] Assuming an average study time of two years, this implies that, at the current rate, nearly 2 per cent of the world's population will pass through university in one of those ten countries as a foreign student. Not all of them will leave as committed globalists, but most will carry with them a set of relationships and perspectives that is far broader than that of their neighbours who stayed at home.[18] So long as that circulation is allowed to continue, it will be possible to continue to progress towards becoming a global nation.

The second area on which globalists should focus is refugees. Allowing migration to prevent the murder, rape or torture of humans is a moral obligation. It is also an issue that requires global co-operation. Refugees are only ever generated where nation-states are unable or unwilling to look after their citizens. If there is any value in a global system, it is to provide a support network of last resort in exactly such cases.

In fact, even in the absence of refugees themselves, the very state failure which risks generating them is a matter in which the global system should intervene – whether to prevent a government from harming its own people or simply to provide additional support to a country that is struggling under the weight of environmental catastrophes or other such pressures. That is why a reformed global system should include a coordinated process for the identification and resettlement of refugees.

The beginnings of such a system is in place, in the form of the United Nations High Commission for Refugees (UNHCR), which channels funding and resources to sustaining the lives of refugees in the world's poorest countries, including through the creation of temporary camps. But these camps are far less temporary than they were designed to be. The average length of time that someone classified as a refugee has been on the UNHCR's books has ranged from between ten and fifteen years since the early 1990s.[19] The UNHCR can provide some food, shelter and other basic items during this time, but it does not have the authority to ensure that these people are integrated into society. Most often, refugees have no political rights and very limited, if any, economic rights in the country where they are forced to live for decades or more.

Global cooperation completely breaks down in two critical areas: firstly, in ensuring reasonable burden-sharing between countries, and secondly, in ensuring the implementation of Article 34 of the UN Convention Relating to the Status of Refugees, which states that host nations must 'as far as possible facilitate the assimilation and naturalization of refugees. They shall in particular make every effort to expedite naturalization proceedings and to reduce as far as possible the charges and costs of such proceedings.'[20]

There is no body capable of enforcing the refugee convention. The UNHCR has supervisory responsibilities but no stick to wield beyond public condemnation. While, in theory, host states are charged with allowing assimilation and naturalization, most of the less wealthy countries, which house the majority of refugees, do not.

Burden-sharing between states is not even mentioned in the refugee convention. But since the existence of refugees is a matter of global concern, it is manifestly unjust to expect the states nearest to a conflagration, which are often the poorest, to shoulder most of the burden. As a result of the lack of any system, the logical course of action for a refugee is to attempt the perilous journey to a wealthy country which does allow naturalization. In the process, they risk their own lives, enrich gangsters who facilitate their journeys and

present a common action problem, where the more generous countries are punished for their generosity by being asked to shoulder a
greater share of the global burden. Unable to make a case for asylum
remotely, refugees are forced to make themselves a 'fact on the
ground' in rich countries by arriving in person – alongside many
more who claim that status but were not in danger of their lives until
they decided to take on the huge risks of undocumented migration.

This status quo has been in tragic operation for decades but has
been thrown into sharper relief since 2015, when illegal migration
into Europe by both genuine refugees and economic migrants claiming that status rapidly increased. In 2015 and 2016 alone, 2.3 million
people entered Europe illegally by crossing the Mediterranean.

Too often, globalists who are comfortable with migration have
pushed for solutions which not only would allow refugees to enter
Europe and receive fair treatment but would also do little to prevent
the mass uncontrolled migration of those who are not genuine refugees. It is, of course, a reasonable position to be in favour of both
refugees and other migrants entering your country. But as we have
seen, one is a moral obligation and the other is up for debate. In
muddying the waters between the two, globalists risk failing to give
the issue of refugees the special status that it deserves.

It is a reasonable compromise with the anti-immigration lobby to
accept that refugee processing should take place outside Europe,
with European countries financially compensating states such as
Tunisia for hosting centres where genuine asylum applicants can be
distinguished from voluntary migrants. The reasonable criticism of
just such a scheme operated by Australia is not that migrants are
processed offshore but that the conditions in which they have been
held, and the time taken to process their application, have not always
been reasonable or humane.

Globalists should push for an offshore solution to be implemented
in a humane setting, with the swift and generous assessment of individual cases and reasonable burden-sharing between European
countries for those refugees who are accepted. At the time of writing,
such a solution was being fiercely contested by many globalists, who
seem far too comfortable with an immigration process that pays no
heed to established law, gives no priority based on need and accepts

into Europe only those who happen to have survived a physically and financially devastating ordeal, at the cost of the lives of many others. This is not how to work towards a world of open borders.

Even if we can build a global nation, perceptions of difference and concerns about strange new neighbours will never completely disappear. No nation has ever fully realized the romantic conception of its founders. The concept of gentrification, and objections to it, arise from the same issues that complicate international migration, now being applied to co-nationals. People from outside moving into an area, breaking up long-established community trust, changing the culture and impacting the economy in uncertain ways: gentrifiers demonstrate that common nationality does not end mutual suspicion.

In China, the *hukou* system has been used to manage some of the tensions arising from internal migration. Huge income gaps across the country have driven hundreds of millions of poor, rural Chinese to migrate to much wealthier cities. While the myth of common nationality has persuaded the native urban populations to tolerate free movement, it has not persuaded them to share public services equally with the newcomers. They have insisted on maintaining privileged access to government services, thereby ensuring that not all the advantages of migration accrue to the migrant. As globalist identity advances, but large income gaps remain, it may be that such a system, allowing free movement but reserving certain privileges to native populations by way of compensation, is a plausible intermediate stage. This is precisely the kind of key-hole solution that free-movement advocates Caplan and Naik suggest.

But such a time is still far off. For now, globalists should play a long game, working to win consensus for their world view. For clues as to when the time is right for more open borders, they should listen to their fellow citizens.

Principle 5: The winners must pay to play

When two classes of citizens do not feel the taxes alike, they cease to have common interests and feelings in common . . . they have no opportunity and no desire to act in concert.

– Alexis de Tocqueville, *The Old Regime and the Revolution*, 1856

For too long, globalization has been explained as a process that inevitably moves people from poorer countries to richer countries, moves manual jobs from richer countries to poorer countries and decreases governments' ability to control the economy – especially when it comes to taxing the ultra-mobile elite. No wonder large sections of the population, especially manual workers in rich countries, have come to see globalization as a threat rather than an opportunity. They see more competition for scarcer jobs in a rapidly changing community that no longer feels like home, while the people gaining most from the global economy contribute less and less, rather than sharing the proceeds of economic growth with people like them who have lost out.

Sadly, the favoured solution among those angered by this narrative is to strengthen the role of governments by undoing much of the global cooperation that seems to be constraining them. Pulling out of trade deals, ending immigration, leaving the European Union, reducing support for the United Nations – such retrograde steps have understandably become popular with people who long for a world in which their elected government is in total control, rather than, as

seems the case, being at the mercy of global business and global institutions. But this would be to kill the goose that laid the golden egg,
ending the unfairness of globalization by dismantling its very ability
to create wealth.

For globalists to change this narrative, they need to demonstrate
not only that the global economic system can create huge gains but
also that those gains can be distributed fairly; not only that there will
be many winners but also that there will be no major losers. That
requires treating taxation – like the wealth which currently escapes
it – as a global issue.

Globally coordinated taxation is needed to address a major challenge that simultaneously undermines faith in both global cooperation
and nation-state governments: the emergence of a seemingly untouch-
able plutocratic elite. This alignment of interests makes tax an issue
on which globalists can profitably focus their energies. Of course,
closing tax loopholes may seem to be against the interests of the very
wealthy, who are currently under-taxed. But they benefit more than
anyone else from the global economic and political system and have
the most to lose if it forfeits the public consent required to keep it in
place. So, in truth, it is in everyone's interest to take action.

Much progress can be made simply by fully implementing the
existing reform agenda, primarily concerned with better information-
sharing, which has been slowly advancing since the financial crisis in
2008.[1] But we should raise the level of ambition by making concerted
calls for the ubiquitous imposition of a minimum annual tax on all
financial assets for those with a net worth above $1 million, set at
perhaps 0.5 per cent. This new tax could be collected by national
governments, who would be free to set its level at a higher rate if
desired but would not be able to set it below the globally agreed
minimum without risking economic isolation.

Such a radical change, which has been proposed in different forms
by several economists in recent years, most famously Thomas Piketty,
is above all about ensuring the fairness of the tax system, not increasing the size of the state.[2] Revenue from the wealth tax would
everywhere be a minority of governments' current revenues. Instead
of boosting state spending, which would of course be an option, the
proceeds might also be used to reduce other taxes, if so desired.

Nation-state governments would retain control of overall fiscal policy but would not be able to provide a haven for international tax exiles.

If we can achieve global coordination and a minimum taxation level for mobile wealth, it will finally be possible to ensure that the world's wealthiest people contribute their fair share. That would boost nation-states, whose governments would have more ability to tax their citizens, but would at the same time increase faith in the possibility of global action. Globalization, for a declining town in middle America, would no longer stand only for job losses, a changing local community and an increasingly distant and wealthy elite. It would mean chasing down the government's rightful dues, no matter where in the world these are hiding, using the proceeds either to increase investment to revitalize that town or reduce taxes on its working-class residents, or both. For that reason, global taxation reform has the potential to be a totemic issue, challenging the anti-globalist narrative that calls globalism a conspiracy of the wealthy against ordinary people and accelerating the path to a global nation.

Those who are reaping astronomical rewards from globalization should be pushing the hardest to salvage faith in the global system, even if it means paying more tax. This is not lost on all of them. Bill Gates and Warren Buffett, two of the richest people in the world, with a combined fortune estimated at $175 billion, have made clear that they believe the current system is unfair. In February 2018, Gates told Fareed Zakaria of CNN: 'I need to pay higher taxes . . . I've paid more taxes, over $10 billion, than anyone else, but the government should require people in my position to pay significantly higher taxes . . . People who are wealthier tend to get dramatically more benefits than the middle class or those who are poorer. It runs counter to the general trend you'd like to see, where the safety net is getting stronger and those at the top are paying higher taxes.'[3]

Building a nation has always involved establishing a system of fair taxation. In Western Europe, where modern nationalism first emerged, the early-modern period saw a shift in the state's revenue model whereby taxes were raised more consistently and in greater quantities. Previously, monarchs had derived the majority of their income from their personal possessions (e.g. rent from land that was directly owned by the king or queen) and levied taxes from the general population only in times of specific need, especially during wars. When the fighting ceased, the taxes lapsed. This system had little need for common solidarity.

But as economies, military technology and interstate competition accelerated, the costs and technical requirements of war increased greatly. From the sixteenth century onwards, Western European economies were made to shoulder a growing tax burden to fund a growing state, eventually including standing armies which were better trained and organized than the periodically raised militias of medieval times.[4] This change has been described as the transition from a 'domain state' (supported by the King's property) to a 'tax state'.[5] Growing bureaucracies busily set about making vast registers of all wealth holdings in each kingdom, as a basis for taxation. Sweden had a particularly accurate record from the sixteenth century. It has even been argued that this detailed Swedish property registry, as much as later socialist ideology, laid the basis for Swedes to be taxed at far higher rates than citizens in other countries, and to support a more egalitarian welfare system, even down to the present day.[6]

One of the ways in which taxation reinforced the development of national sentiment was through public resistance to the levies, which pressured governments to act less as absolute rulers and more as representatives of the people. For example, in both England and France a tradition emerged whereby new taxes could be imposed by the King only with the approval of 'parliament'.[7] In neither country did the parliament represent the 'nation' in the modern sense. But the requirement for parliamentary approval did mean that monarchs were forced to obtain some broader consent for taxation.

It is interesting to note the contrast with China, where there was a long-established 'tax state' and a strong Chinese identity. But China in the early-modern period did not experience the intense interstate competition that in Europe greatly raised the costs of warfare. Chinese taxation levels were not on an upward trend.[8] It may not be entirely coincidental to this that the Chinese government did not in that period move from absolute rule towards the premise of the sovereignty of the people.[9]

The cases of Britain, France and the United States of America demonstrate how the establishment of fair taxation was central to the development of nationalism.[10] Of the three, Britain entered the age of nationalism with the most representative government and was therefore able to raise large sums in taxation without suffering revolts. Throughout the eighteenth century, the British government spent every year between 8 per cent and 10 per cent of the national income, mostly to pay directly for the military, or to pay off debts accrued during previous military campaigns. This was a very high tax burden for the time, but the parliamentary system, through which voters were able to lobby for their interests and appeal against perceived unfairness, meant that taxes were accepted and paid with great reliability. This 'fiscal consent' (broad acceptance of taxation) allowed Britain to survive the transition into the nationalist era of the late eighteenth and nineteenth centuries with less disruption than many other countries.[11]

France was an entirely different story. Its monarchs had clung on to absolute rule, partly by giving in to some of the demands of powerful nobles, including exemptions from most forms of taxation. This meant that the tax system let off many of those who were most able to pay, while also appearing less fair to those who did contribute, thereby raising less money but with louder opposition. Adam Smith, in 1776, marvelled at France's less fortunate position:

> The French system of taxation seems, in every respect, inferior to the British . . .
>
> In 1765 and 1766, the whole revenue paid into the treasury of France . . . did not amount to fifteen millions sterling; not the half of what might have been expected had the people contributed in the same proportion to their numbers as the people of Great Britain. The people of France, however, it is generally acknowledged, are much more oppressed by taxes than the people of Great Britain.[12]

A decade later, that system had collapsed. It has been long established that the perceived unfairness of the tax system, combined with its inability to raise sufficient funds, were among the primary causes of the French Revolution, which sought to reset the constitutional basis for government and emancipate the *Grande Nation*.[13] While hugely disruptive, this confrontation ultimately left France with a fairer tax system mediated through more representative institutions, allowing tax rates to be raised considerably in the decades that followed.

The United States of America is another story of a nation whose common consciousness was sparked by rebellion against unfair taxes. As any American high-school student knows, one of the founding principles of their country is 'no taxation without representation'. In the first century after being established, Britain's American colonies maintained, on the whole, a British, or English, identity. This changed when, in the 1760s, the British government began to set high excise taxes on goods, including tea. Without the parliamentary representation that allowed such disputes to be resolved in Britain, the myth of common nationhood snapped. By 1789, a new independent nation had formed under the world's first written constitution, beginning with the pre-eminently nationalist phrase, 'We, the people . . .'

The tension between taxation and representation did not stop there. An influential trend of thinking on public consent since the 1960s, the Virginia School states that any given constitutional arrangement will have associated with it a maximum level of taxation which it can extract with the consent of the people. Politicians will over time find ways to increase taxation until it reaches that maximum, at which it must stay, unless a new constitutional arrangement enabling a consensus for higher taxes can be found.[14] While not without its critics, this remains an elegant analysis of the process which led from medieval absolute monarchies living off their private income through to today's nation-states, which in rich countries tend to have a universal franchise and taxation exceeding a third of national income, primarily spent on education, health and benefits.

These changes have also increased the expectation of contribution from the wealthiest. In most early societies, the most powerful people were able to exempt themselves from some or all taxation.[15] In the era of nationalism, it became important that everyone contributed. But before the twentieth century, the expectation was of a proportional, not redistributive, burden. To Adam Smith, it was obvious that: 'The subjects of every state ought to contribute towards the support of the government, as nearly as possible, in proportion to their respective abilities; that is, in proportion to the revenue which they respectively enjoy under the protection of the state.'[16] The twentieth century, along with the universal franchise in many countries, and the Bolshevik Revolution in Russia, brought the expectation that taxation should be progressive, reducing the inequalities created by capitalism. In communist countries this came in the form of a once-and-for-all confiscation of wealth and the nationalization of all property. In market economies, the change was less pronounced but it became almost everywhere an expectation of government that they would use their powers to redistribute at least some of the nation's wealth from the richest to the poorest. Indeed, for much of the twentieth century, even capitalist Britain and America had punitive taxes on large incomes and estates, with a 98 per cent top rate of tax on both in the UK in the 1940s and 1970s, and an 80 per cent top rate of income tax in the US in the aftermath of the Great Depression.[17]

The last decades of globalization have threatened to undo the positive cycle of increased taxation and increased representation. Today, the world resembles pre-Revolution France: exemptions for the elite and anger from the masses. The unfairness of taxation is threatening the national compact nearly everywhere.

Several recent studies have tried to quantify the scale of the problem. According to the relatively conservative estimates of Gabriel Zucman, 8 per cent of all global wealth is stashed in tax havens.[18] He reasonably guesses that only 20 per cent of this wealth is declared to tax authorities in the countries of citizenship of its owners. This wealth, the vast majority of which is held in financial instruments, is owned by a complex web of shell companies whose beneficial ownership (i.e. the people whose money it really is) is entirely hidden. Of course, the wealth has not in most cases actually been physically transferred to tax havens. A French person, for example, can own shares in a French company but entirely avoid paying French taxes on that holding because they have created an appropriately obscure paper trail that winds its imaginary course through Luxembourg, Switzerland and the British Virgin Islands.

There are perhaps eighty such tax havens which have opted to use their sovereignty as an export-generating asset. That is to say, they use the fact that they are an independent law-setting entity within a world of nation-states governed by an international system to set taxes and transparency at zero, in order to attract to themselves a lucrative business in managing those assets. These havens, such as Luxembourg, the Cayman Islands and Panama, have such small populations that the relatively small revenue in services and real estate generated by attracting so much untaxed wealth is enough to maintain them at a relatively high standard of living.[19] But the tax havens themselves attract only a modest portion of the windfall from unpaid tax – with small populations and vast wealth flowing through them (if only on paper), that is all they need. The big winners are the owners of untaxed assets. The losers include everyone who does not hide their assets abroad and is not a citizen of a tax haven; that is to say, almost all humans.

Some regions are affected more than others. Africa, the world's poorest continent, with the lowest tax income and the greatest need for investment, had fully 30 per cent of its private wealth hidden in tax havens. In the United States, the proportion for personal wealth is much smaller, but fully 55 per cent of corporations' overseas profits are held in tax havens. The only method that the US government has found in recent years to repatriate this money is to offer occasional tax holidays – effectively amnesties whereby companies can for a limited period bring this money back to the US while paying little or no tax on it. Such a move was implemented by George W. Bush from 2004 to 2005. Donald Trump's administration is planning something similar.[20]

How much tax is avoided in this way? Zucman calculates that, according to current tax laws, around $200 billion in annual tax revenue is being illegally withheld from governments by private individuals using tax havens. Of that money, $78 billion is owed each year to EU governments alone, representing nearly half of the EU's annual budget. In the US, where only $35 billion is estimated to be lost by private use of tax havens, a massive $130 billion is lost to the Treasury every year by companies shifting profits to low- or no-tax jurisdictions. But it is in the poorest countries that the loss of tax revenue is most severe, not only because they need the money (across

Africa, only 35 per cent of people have access to electricity, and the annual gap in infrastructure spending compared to what is required to keep pace with other continents is estimated at $48 billion per year)[21] but also because governments are less able to tax the broad mass of the population, some of whom earn little more than subsistence income, while others work in the informal sector and so are harder to tax.

Globally, an estimated $600 billion in corporation tax is lost every year, of which a third is owed to developing countries.[22] Combined with the $200 billion in lost personal taxes, that adds up to around 4 per cent of all taxes collected worldwide. That money could do a lot of good. It is more than four times the total aid budgets of all donor countries[23] and is almost double the total annual remittances that are sent by diasporas back to low- and middle-income countries.[24] If all of that money was collected by governments and spent on education, it would increase the world's public education spend by 20 per cent. However, the true tax losses due to the current system – or lack of a system – are far higher. That is because taxes on wealth and corporate profits are far lower than they would be if governments were able to set them democratically.

It is a well-established fact that wealth and corporation taxes have been subject to intense downward pressure in recent decades, as wealthy individuals and companies are increasingly able to choose where they pay tax.[25] As the global movement of capital has become increasingly easy, corporation tax has declined. The average rates of corporation tax across OECD countries fell from 41 per cent in 1981 to 23 per cent in 2014. Meanwhile, US multinationals' effective tax rates across fifty countries (taxes paid as a proportion of income in that jurisdiction) was just 33 per cent in 1983 and fell to just 18.5 per cent in 2011.[26] In America, revenues from corporation tax fell from 5 per cent of GDP in the 1950s to 2 per cent in 2019.[27]

The factors driving these falling tax rates are clear to anyone watching political debates around the time corporate taxes are lowered: in the battle to attract business, each reduction in tax by another country piles on pressure to reduce one's own rates. The rates are not truly set by democratic decision-making but through a 'race to the bottom' where each country struggles to maintain their share of a shrinking pie. Meanwhile, citizens demand more taxes on the rich but are told by governments that this is not something they can deliver.

The case for corporate tax cuts is never about fairness or the need for a smaller state. It is about keeping up with other countries, as George Osborne told the UK Parliament soon after becoming Chancellor of the Exchequer in 2010: 'Corporation tax rates are compared around the world, and low rates act as adverts for the countries that introduce them ... Our current rate of 28p is looking less and less competitive.'[28] What followed, under Osborne's Chancellorship and continuing under his successor, Philip Hammond, was a series of massive reductions in corporation tax, which fell from 28 per cent in 2010 to 19 per cent in 2017 and is due to fall further, to just 17 per cent by 2020. If Osborne had remained as Chancellor, the rate would be lower still. Again citing the need to be 'competitive', he called in 2016 for rates to be lowered to 15 per cent in the aftermath of the Brexit vote but was removed from office by the new Prime Minister Theresa May before he could implement the policy.[29]

By contrast, the United States had kept relatively high corporation taxes on paper but in practice allowed foreign profits either not to be taxed (when they are held abroad), or to be taxed at exceptionally low rates when repatriated during 'tax holidays' (President Bush's tax holiday set the rate at just 5.45 per cent). In December 2017, Donald Trump's administration resolved this paradox by bringing the tax rate down to 21 per cent, thereby giving in to corporations' de facto threat: if you keep your tax rates high, we will keep our profits abroad.

The threat was a real one. In Britain, as the corporate tax rate plummeted, the revenue from corporation tax soared, rising from £36 billion in 2010 to £56 billion in 2017.[30] This was naturally declared a great victory for the tax-cut policy. But a 55 per cent jump in receipts after the rate dropped by 30 per cent is highly suspicious and cannot easily be explained by Britain 'attracting business' in a meaningful way. Much of the increase in receipts is likely to have been caused by multinational companies choosing to pay a higher proportion of their taxes in the UK by moving profits between their subsidiaries through what is known as transfer pricing (one subsidiary 'sells' physical or intellectual property to another, allowing more profits to show up in the 'selling' subsidiary than in the 'buying' one). Where possible, companies ensure assets are owned by subsidiaries in tax havens, which is why, for example, Google's search algorithm is based in Bermuda. Google's Bermuda subsidiary then charges its other subsidiaries in higher-tax jurisdictions for the right to use the algorithm. This ensures that the untaxed Bermuda subsidiary is highly profitable, and higher-tax subsidiaries have fewer profits on their books.

Not all assets are like intellectual property, which is so immaterial that it can be transferred to a Caribbean island at the click of a button. But by carefully managing staffing levels and the prices charged by one subsidiary to another, even more tangible businesses can ensure they pay more profits in countries with lower taxes, such as the UK. That means some more income for the low-tax country, but much less income for everyone else. But the strategy of cutting tax rates and paradoxically increasing government revenue works only in the short term. Now that the United States has lowered its tax rates to levels similar to those of the UK, it is likely that Britain's recent boost to tax receipts will dry up and both countries will be left with low tax rates and low government revenue. Soon enough, a major economy may follow Ireland in setting rates much lower still (Ireland's corporate tax rate is just 12 per cent, but it is such a small country that there is a limit to how much profits can be made to surface there). At that point, both the UK and the US will again seem to have 'uncompetitive' rates, as corporate profits magically show up in the newly low-tax economy. And so the 'race to the bottom' continues.

If corporation tax has seen a steady decline in the age of mobile capital, personal wealth taxes have all but disappeared. This trend began in Europe, the home of most wealth taxes, with Germany and Denmark both abolishing in 1997 what had been significant taxes on net wealth above a certain threshold.[31] Finland, Luxembourg and Iceland abolished wealth taxes in 2006 (although Iceland temporarily reinstated theirs due to fiscal difficulties from 2010 to 2014), followed by Sweden in 2007. The following year, Spain abolished its wealth tax, although this was reinstated in 2010 due to the fiscal constraints of a worsening economy.[32]

In recent years, more countries have followed suit, including India, which in 2016 ended a tax that had commanded 1 per cent annually on all net personal wealth exceeding Rs. 3 million ($44,000).[33] But perhaps the most devastating blow to global wealth taxes was when in 2017 President Macron ended France's 'wealth solidarity tax', which had covered all net wealth above €1.3 million and raised €5.5 billion per year. Macron replaced it with a 'non-mobile wealth tax' covering only real estate.[34]

Until 2017, France had been the only G7 economy to impose a significant tax covering all the assets of its richest citizens, including financial instruments. To some, it was continuing proof that such a policy was possible in a world of globalized capital. But to others, including its new president, its lone stance in taxing financial assets was costing it business and investment.[35] To a president desperate to resurrect France's entrepreneurial spirit, there seemed little choice: he must encourage flighty financial assets to remain in France by limiting the wealth tax to buildings, which are much harder to haul off to the Caribbean. In the current global tax environment, that might seem like a sensible policy. But it comes with a social cost, introducing the kind of exemption for the privileged elite that the French Revolution was designed to end. The name of the new tax is instructive. The word 'non-mobile' was added. The word 'solidarity' was removed.

So it is clear that governments are being forced to reduce or remove taxes on corporate profits and personal wealth not by the democratic will of their citizens but by 'tax competition' with other countries. I have already argued in Chapter 5 that nation-states should continue to be able to choose their own internal arrangement so long as they do not harm each other. But the current system does allow one country's tax regime to harm that of another. If Country A decides to levy heavy corporate taxes and spends some of them on providing an environment which they hope is more amenable to business, it is reasonable for companies to be presented a choice as to whether to do business there, or in Country B, where there are lower taxes and less expense on the items which Country A hoped would be attractive. But that is not how tax competition actually works today.

Multinational companies do business everywhere, taking advantage of the improved business environment provided by government expenditure on infrastructure, the rule of law and education, but they then choose to pay taxes only in the low-tax jurisdictions. A recent example came from Amazon, which had vast revenues from its booming UK business, reaching £8.7 billion in the tax year 2017–18. However, only £2 billion of those revenues flowed to its UK registered subsidiary, which paid tax of just £1.7 million on declared profits of just £79 million. The remaining £6.7 billion of Amazon's UK revenues flowed to another subsidiary based in Luxembourg, a tax haven. Amazon is not legally obliged to reveal how much tax was paid on that amount. We can bet that it was very little indeed.

In a cruel twist, globalization has robbed governments of the ability to tax the wealthiest people, just as it has greatly increased their ability to generate wealth by accessing global markets and workforces. That was already the case before 2008, but the unfairness was exacerbated by policy decisions taken in the aftermath of the Global Financial Crisis. Bail-outs of the banking system, followed by years of rock-bottom interest rates and quantitative easing programmes instituted by the world's two biggest economies – the US and the EU – first shored up, and then inflated global asset prices and thereby increased inequality. The inequality effect of asset price rises is particularly pronounced because wealth is, and has always been, much more unequally distributed than income, as demonstrated by Thomas Piketty.[36]

These asset-inflating policies, described by John Lanchester as 'both necessary and a disaster',[37] may have been required to avoid economic meltdown but they also implied a huge transfer of money from poor and middle-class taxpayers to those who were already wealthy. The result has been reduced government spending ('austerity') and spiralling inequality within many countries,[38] leading to real public anger. That anger is a threat both to nation-states and to the global system. Many millions of people feel that the masters of the global economy, in cahoots with their own governments, have robbed them of the income, the security and the prospects they had expected while pocketing the proceeds of capitalism for themselves. And as tends to be the case with public anger and frustration, it is not always aimed at the right targets. Donald Trump, in a brilliant sleight of hand, has convinced millions of Americans that the solution to these problems is for their country to act more unilaterally and reduce taxes on the wealthy – exactly the opposite of the global co-ordination to tax wealth that is needed.

This dangerous public anger towards inequality and the impunity of the wealthy is a truly worldwide phenomenon, as we saw with the 2015 Panama Papers scandal. Prime ministers fell in New Zealand and (eventually) Pakistan; associates of Russia's President Putin and the brother-in-law of China's President Xi, along with scores of other members of the global political and business elite, were named as owning secret wealth-holding companies. We have entered a phase, not only in rich countries but also in Brazil, Pakistan, the Philippines and across the world, where the surest way to win votes is to vow to tear down the current system and jail those who profit from it.[39] Even in one-party China, the leadership has found it necessary to present itself as a ruthless scourge of corrupt officials in an attempt to appease anger against soaring inequality and elite impunity.

None of this anger is reducing inequality or forcing the richest to pay taxes. Wealth inequality continues to rise, year after year, as documented by Oxfam, which calculated that 80 per cent of the new wealth generated in 2017 went to the richest 1 per cent of people, while the 3.5 billion people in the bottom 50 per cent of global wealth saw no net increase at all.[40] Meanwhile, Gabriel Zucman finds that the amount of private wealth held in tax havens has soared since 2008.[41] And as Branko Milanovic warns, 'a very high inequality eventually becomes unsustainable, but it does not go down by itself; rather, it generates processes, like wars, social strife, and revolutions, that lower it'.[42]

The surest way to avoid such drastic outcomes is to learn the lessons of nation-building in the past. We need to realign the constitutional arrangements to suit the modern economy. To Adam Smith in the late eighteenth century it was obvious that 'every great country [is] necessarily the best and most extensive market for the greater part of the productions of its own industry'.[43] In the twenty-first century, we have allowed economic activity to become global, while maintaining a country-by-country tax system better suited to Adam Smith's time. Only by reimagining taxation as a global activity can we reverse the process by which the new aristocracy has won exemptions for itself at the cost of the system's stability.

Thankfully, momentum is building, because many governments increasingly realize that they cannot assuage public anger without acting in concert. While they continue the lose–lose 'race to the bottom' – responding to the pressures of the current system by lowering taxes on wealth and corporate income – they are also working together on changing that system. The four most important actors to date have been the United States, the EU (including the UK), the OECD (a Paris-based organization with thirty-six members, most of whom are high-income countries) and the G20 (the club of the world's twenty biggest economies).

So far, action has been mainly restricted to increasing transparency and information-sharing. That may seem like small-fry, but it should not be underestimated. For corporate tax, one of the biggest issues is that multinationals present each jurisdiction a tax return relating only to the subsidiary operating in that jurisdiction. The financials of each subsidiary, as we have seen, include imaginary 'buying' and 'selling' between the different subsidiaries. So prominent is this kind of imaginary trading that it represents as much as 60 per cent of all international trade, according to the UN.[44] There is plenty of opportunity within this fog to move profits to where it best suits the company. To try to combat this, the OECD and G20 are working with 116 tax authorities, with mandates covering 95 per cent of the global economy, to close these loopholes, in what they call Base Erosion and Profit Shifting (BEPS). In July 2018, the OECD claimed the BEPS project had already brought $108.6 billion of revenue to tax authorities and had changed the behaviour of corporations, which were already 'taking pro-active steps aimed at aligning their tax structures with their real economic activity'.

This level of global action on corporate tax represents a real step change. But as Amazon's UK tax contributions demonstrate, the behaviour change is nowhere near complete. We need to remove the pretence that multinational companies are in fact a collection of independent subsidiaries which trade with each other. This is a result of trying to fit the square peg of a global economy into the round hole of over two hundred independent tax jurisdictions.

Instead, the world's governments should apply the same philosophy as the United States does when approaching corporate tax across its fifty states. Each state has its own corporation tax rates, incentives and rules. However, the amount of profits subject to taxes in each state is not decided in a secretive free-for-all. Instead, they use a system called Unitary Taxation with Formula Allocation (UT-FA). Each corporation submits consolidated accounts for the entire United States, showing what their revenues, costs and assets are in each state. A formula is then applied to determine, based on those factors, how much of the company's profits should be attributed to its activities in each state. Each state's tax policies are then applied to the portion of profit that is allocated to that state. Applying this system to global corporate taxation is eminently achievable, by building on and expanding the unprecedented level of cooperation already taking place on this issue. Pushing their governments to take this additional step should be a focus of globalists' efforts.

Information-sharing should also be extended to include personal wealth. As we saw, the tax-states of Europe which laid the foundation for modern nations began by making detailed registries of who owned what. They did that at a time when almost all wealth consisted in land and the immobile improvements to it (irrigation ditches, buildings, and so on). The way to start updating our fiscal constitution to match the global economy is by creating a global wealth register covering all forms of property, including financial instruments.[45]

The United States led the way in 2010 with its Foreign Account Tax Compliance Act (FATCA), which forces any non-US financial institution which conducts business with the United States to reveal all assets held by US citizens and residents, including those owned through a web of secretive shell companies. Importantly, FATCA imposes big penalties on institutions which do not comply, withholding 30 per cent of all US-based payments to those institutions. Given the size of the US economy, few financial institutions can afford to escape this by avoiding doing business in the US. To ensure non-compliant institutions are exposed, the US Treasury offers cash rewards to whistleblowers that can run to more than $100 million. As a result, vast swathes of information on previously undeclared holdings of US citizens have come to light.

FATCA has been an important demonstration exercise, revealing that bank secrecy can be dented even by the US acting on its own. But the only beneficiary of this information is the US Treasury, which is under no obligation to share information with other countries, and which does not demand information on the assets of other countries' citizens. Over the long term, even US citizens who want to hide their wealth will be able to do so by using a growing number of smaller investment vehicles which avoid doing business with the United States. This will be increasingly easy to do as the US economy becomes an ever-smaller proportion of the world economy (it has already shrunk from 40 per cent in 1960 to 34 per cent in 1985 and just 22 per cent in 2014).[46]

The start made by FATCA needs to be scaled up to be a global system. The OECD and G20 have made strides in this regard, but their efforts are mainly centred on information-sharing between tax authorities rather than the creation of a single global database of assets. A particularly encouraging step is the recent adoption by over fifty countries of the OECD's 'automatic sharing of information' protocol, which requires tax authorities to share details on assets held by citizens of other countries with those countries' tax authorities immediately they are identified and without any specific requests being made.

These efforts laid the basis for a global asset register to be collected. But many political obstacles to that process remain. There are reasonable fears about data security: while at one end of the scale, some, like Gabriel Zucman, believe that such a register should be open to the public, privacy activists at the other end worry that even governments confidentially sharing information with each other is not a sufficient protection.

This transparency question is an important one, but it cannot be allowed to stand in the way of an effective tax system. The way to stop such a register being used by criminals for kidnap and extortion is by building strong societies and effective policing, both of which are improved when the wealthiest people pay their taxes. The reason that the wealthiest people in most places are not currently subject to such injustices is not because there is no public information about their exact wealth. There are many people who are already well known to have significant wealth. Most of them do not have body-guards. While the publicly quoted figures on their net worth are currently only journalists' estimates, an extra degree of accuracy on this public knowledge would be unlikely to radically change the risk to their safety (assuming they are not revealed to be crooks). Nevertheless, there are places in the world where the wealthy are subject to great risks. To mitigate this, implementation could be gradual, for example initially allowing access to the database only to tax authorities who can demonstrate sufficient confidentiality guarantees and making public only the information on the citizens of countries where the risk to wealthy people is at a tolerable level.

Such a global wealth register is a necessary step, but it is not sufficient. Although they are not as mobile as their assets, which can be moved at the click of a button, wealthy people are only a plane ride away from moving to a low-tax or no-tax country. They do not face many visa controls because such countries are keen to attract them as residents and even citizens. Many of the wealthiest people are already resident in tax havens. In a world where all wealth was recorded and available to tax authorities, countries which agreed not to tax it would become increasingly attractive. The race to the bottom which we have seen in operation would continue.

The assets of wealthy people translate ultimately into real economic activity in major economies, activity that can happen only because those economies have the kind of infrastructure, rule of law and social solidarity which fair taxation is needed to provide. So wealthy people living in tax havens, even if they do not use roads and hospitals paid for by taxes, are free-riding on countries which levy taxes because, without them, their financial assets would plummet in value. That is why it should be established that all countries must levy a tax on net wealth, including financial wealth, and that this tax should nowhere fall below a minimum agreed level.

My proposal is that all people with net worth above $1 million should face a minimum wealth tax of 0.5 per cent per year on their net worth over that threshold. According to Credit Suisse's analysis, in 2017 this would have applied to 36 million people, of whom 75 per cent live in Europe and North America. Their collective holdings are estimated at $127 trillion, meaning that a 0.5 per cent wealth tax, after the personal allowance of $1 million per person was excluded, would raise $455 billion, adding more than 2 per cent to global tax revenue.[47]

Given the geographical inequality of wealth distribution, each country would receive a very different amount. Just over 50 per cent of the money raised – about $229 billion – would go to the US Treasury, collected from America's 15.4 million millionaires. China would receive 5 per cent of the total, raising about $26 billion from its 2 million millionaires. Norway, a wealthy country but with just 5 million people, would receive 0.5 per cent of the total, raising around $2.3 billion from its 200,000 millionaires.

Globally, the tax would affect the richest 0.5 per cent of the world's population – those dollar millionaires who owned 45.9 per cent of all wealth, in 2017. However, most of these 36 million people have wealth only a little above $1 million and would pay very little in tax. Someone with net wealth of $1,200,000 would pay just $1,000 per year. Most of the burden would be borne by those who have made astronomical fortunes from the global system, often helped by government policies that inflated asset prices. It is eminently reasonable for governments to implement countervailing policies to recover a small part of those gains for the common use. Indeed, a rate of 0.5 per cent is very modest. The global real average return on private capital in the twentieth century has been 5 per cent.[48] So, on average, the tax would take just 10 per cent of the income from capital. While some assets will of course perform less well, this tax will almost nowhere eat into the capital stock of reasonably invested wealth (naturally, there is a great value for the economy in adding an incentive to make sure that wealth is reasonably invested).

For some people, this proposal will not go nearly far enough. While ensuring a minimum contribution from all millionaires, my proposal would not achieve real redistribution. Historian Samuel Moyn makes a powerful case that the international community's focus on human rights has allowed us to ignore the problem of inequality. He maintains that global justice requires measures to make people more equal, not just to protect them from the most abject misery.[49]

If you view the world as a single nation, Moyn's case is appealing. But global solidarity has not progressed far enough. Put simply, most people in rich countries want everyone to have basic human rights but they do not want the poorer countries to catch up with them. They want to maintain global inequalities. Within nation-states, there are different views on how redistributive government should be. The global system cannot dictate to nation-states that they must implement a policy of redistribution. However, just as the consensus within nation-states has developed over time, so a growing globalist identity can eventually lead to efforts for a more equal world. Establishing the principle of globally coordinated tax can be a step towards that goal.

What to do with $455 billion raised by a millionaires wealth tax? I propose a split between global and nation-state priorities. All the wealth tax would be collected by nation-state governments, but the expected contribution of each country to the global system – through foreign aid – would be calculated as half of the wealth tax accruing to that country. This would increase only slightly the funding available to tackle the Global Goals (foreign aid currently stands at around $200 billion), but it would substantially improve the basis for calculating it.

Currently, rich countries pay for foreign aid out of general taxation, which means that the taxes paid by the very poorest Americans, French and Chinese go towards helping people in other countries. Unsurprisingly, foreign aid – and the global solidarity it implies – is unpopular among many of them. They do not see themselves as wealthy, and in many countries they have seen their living standards, as well as government services, decline in recent years. They argue that their taxes, instead of going towards global development, should be spent to help those in need back home. What's more, rich countries give foreign aid, but rich people from poorer countries have no obligation to contribute, even though it is countries like theirs that benefit most from it. Calculating foreign aid as a proportion of the proceeds of a millionaires wealth tax would present the opportunity to change this narrative. Every millionaire worldwide would be expected to contribute to tackling poverty and climate change, no matter what country he or she was from. No one else's taxes would be called on for this task, even if they happened to live in a rich country. Global development could become a project of real global solidarity, with the richest helping the poorest, shedding the post-colonial narrative in which some countries 'give' and others 'receive'.

For some very generous countries this would mean their minimum expected contributions to global development would decrease. Norway's foreign aid budget in 2018 was $4.4 billion,[50] four times what they would be asked to contribute under my proposed system. It is unlikely that these generous countries, which are already contributing more than international expectations, would reduce their aid spending. That generosity over and above the expectation on millionaires is to be welcomed. However, for other countries, contributions would have to go up. Most significant would be the increase for the United States, which is currently the least generous of the world's wealthiest countries. Half of the wealth tax paid by America's 15.4 million millionaires would amount to $130 billion. Coincidentally, that is almost exactly what the US is expected to pay currently, according to the UN's target of rich countries contributing 0.7 per cent of gross national income (GNI) to foreign aid. Several countries, including the UK, are already that generous. In reality, however, the US's aid budget for 2019 is $39.3 billion, just 0.2 per cent of GNI. Explaining America's contribution as a portion of the proceeds of a tax on millionaires would be a better rationale for calling on it to contribute more.

The portion of the millionaires tax spent on global development would be expected but voluntary. It could be encouraged through increased voting rights at the United Nations. The remaining half of the wealth tax could be used by governments as they pleased. Whether it was used to reduce other taxes or to improve public services, the biggest beneficiaries would be the less wealthy people in the richest countries. If communicated and implemented in the right way, this holds the opportunity to win round one of the groups most opposed to global cooperation to the view that it can be made to serve them.

To implement these proposals, there are some technical hurdles that must be crossed, but by far the biggest element is political will. If the majority of citizens in a large number of countries were calling loudly for their governments to make this happen, it would not take long for UT-FA, a global wealth register and a minimum wealth tax for millionaires to be put into place. From a technical point of view, the real hard work would be in creating the global wealth register, which, as discussed, is necessary whether or not a global minimum wealth tax was implemented.[51]

Having created such a register, which could be housed in an existing or new international institution, a monitoring system would be needed to verify through periodic reviews that the minimum tax amount was being collected from those people on the wealth register with assets above $1 million. Again, such monitoring would be straightforward from a technical point of view if the political will existed.

Finally, there is the issue of what to do with offenders. No global agreement which individual tax havens or politicians stand to benefit from flouting can be implemented without the threat of consequences for ignoring it. Here again, political will is the key. The interconnect-edness of the global economy means that, for every country, to be entirely economically isolated would carry far heavier costs than the gains of maintaining the status of a tax haven. If the world decides that the rules of the global economy include making sure wealth is taxed and excludes those who do not play by those rules, few countries would choose to be outside the tent. Those that did would no longer be attractive places for the wealthy to relocate to, removing their incentive to keep up their stubborn resistance.

Throughout history, nations have been born from popular protests that insist taxes are fair and that they be spent on the right things. The dazzling achievements of a globalized economy have presented the opportunity for the ultimate nation to be imagined. But as long as that system provides opt-outs for the elite and underinvests in the very poorest, as well as the less wealthy citizens of the richest countries, we will continue to stand on the edge of a precipice. People all over the world are angry about inequality and tax avoidance, but they are yet to be convinced that a global system controlled by the winners can bring any solutions to these problems. Instead, the case is often being won by politicians spinning narratives of isolation and xenophobia. The primary obstacle to generating the political will to implement real global tax reform is the short-sightedness of wealthy globalists who believe they can continue to have their cake and eat it. They must learn the lesson of the French Revolution and share the cake more widely before it is swept away.

Principle 6: The 'rules-based system' needs better rules

For I dipt into the future, far as human eye could see,
Saw the Vision of the world, and all the wonder
  that would be . . .
Till the war-drum throbb'd no longer, and the
  battle-flags were furl'd
In the Parliament of man, the Federation of the world.
There the common sense of most shall hold a fretful
  realm in awe,
And the kindly earth shall slumber, lapt in
  universal law.

> – Alfred, Lord Tennyson,
> 'Locksley Hall', 1842

When the poem quoted above was first written, in the mid-nineteenth century, the idea of a 'parliament of man' seemed little more than the dream of a romantic poet, perhaps the Victorian equivalent of John Lennon's 'Imagine'. One hundred years later, as the Second World War came to a close, it was less absurd. US President Harry Truman is said to have carried with him since his youth those words from Tennyson's 'Locksley Hall', on a folded sheet of paper in his pocket. They were still in his pocket during the tense negotiations through which the United Nations was born.[1]

At that heady time, global cooperation was a bipartisan issue in America. While President Roosevelt was planning with his wartime allies to create a United Nations, Wendell Willkie, his defeated Republican opponent in the 1940 presidential election, was touring the US advocating the same cause.[2] This was no elite globalist plot; the politicians were aligned with public opinion. Polls showed that more than 80 per cent of Americans wanted the US to participate in a world assembly with the power to assure the peace.[3]

But Truman, who after Roosevelt's sudden death had to lead the 1945 San Francisco conference that created the UN, stopped short of championing Tennyson's 'Federation of the world'. Instead, a more modest plan was agreed, whereby individual nation-states would maintain complete sovereignty. Instead of a global government with enforcement power, they would create a secretariat, the United Nations Organization, to manage their joint deliberations and carry out jointly agreed projects. All major decisions would be taken by the nation-states themselves, through a system of voting which allowed, through the design of the powerful Security Council, the five most powerful states on the winning side a veto over the use of force. The secretariat would be headed not by a president or chief executive, but by a Secretary-General. It has been a common saying ever since that the person sought for the post should be 'more a secretary than a general'.

It seems remarkable enough that even this relatively modest global infrastructure was built. Throughout the Cold War, its goal of ensuring consensus and peace between the great powers seemed totally unachievable. After the fall of Communism in Eastern Europe, hopes were again revived that the United Nations could stand at the centre of a non-violent world system characterized by joint action, even on that thorniest of issues – the use of force. Between 1991 and 1993 the UN Security Council, previously deadlocked by the perpetual vetoes of rival members, passed an astonishing 185 resolutions, more than four times the rate at which it managed to produce agreement in the previous forty-six years.[4] In 2005, there was even a major attempt to make the UN more relevant, representative and fair, including an enlargement of the Security Council.[5]

We live in more sober times. Donald Trump has been clear that he wants America to pursue its interests bilaterally, rather than through organizations such as the UN, which he has threatened with massive budget cuts. His persistent refusal to reappoint judges to the World Trade Organization's Dispute Settlement Board, at the time of writing, brought the WTO close to collapse.[6] The most notoriously hostile and uncompromising US Ambassador to the UN of recent times, John Bolton, who is credited more than anyone else with torpedoing the 2005 proposal for Security Council reform, is now US National Security Advisor. Russia is seeking its own geographical sphere of influence and is prepared to veto any UN action that might threaten it. Even Japan, historically a staunch supporter of multilateral action and global institutions, is building up its military and calling into question the relevance of the United Nations if it is not reformed.[7]

In this context, it is easy to forget that after the Second World War the strength of feeling in support of an effective global system was such that many people across the world were bitterly disappointed that the United Nations' original design did not go even further in binding the world's peoples together. Chastened by the failure of the League of Nations, which sprang up in the aftermath of the First World War, to prevent a second global conflict just a few years later, there was popular support for an organization with real powers.

Despite the Realpolitik which dictated the final agreement in San Francisco, President Truman, whose administration was by far the biggest contributor to the text of the final document, always saw the 1945 agreement as the first stage in a process that would lead to even more unity. In his closing speech at the San Francisco conference, in which fifty states had worked for weeks to hash out an agreed UN Charter, he compared their agreement to the first steps in creating the United States:

> The Constitution of my own country came from a Convention which – like this one – was made up of delegates with many different views ... When it was adopted, no one regarded it as a perfect document. But it grew and developed and expanded. And upon it there was built a bigger, a better, a more perfect union. This Charter, like our own Constitution, will be expanded and improved as time goes on.[8]

For many who believe in the UN system, their greatest hope now is simply that it survives its current travails intact. Indeed, when I spoke to Lord Malloch-Brown, formerly Deputy Secretary-General of the UN, Vice-president of the World Bank and head of the United

Nations Development Programme (UNDP), he was gloomy about the prospects of reform. He had been heavily involved in attempts to update the UN system in 2005; his book on UN reform, *The Unfinished Global Revolution*, was published in 2011.[9] Looking back, he sees the two main institutional changes that were made on his watch – the creation of the Peacekeeping Council and the Human Rights Council – as disappointments. But even more disappointing was the failure to agree any changes to the most powerful, and the most unfairly designed, of all UN bodies: the Security Council. According to Malloch-Brown, 'the unreformed security council has dropped back to one of its most dismal levels of performance at any time in the UN's history. But in truth, whatever momentum there was or groundswell of support in favour of reform has dissipated. It's dissipated because it's got lost in the broader crisis of globalization.'[10]

Despite this gloomy outlook, Lord Malloch-Brown is far from giving up. He's still convinced that 'the arguments in favour of global integration will prevail, but it's going to be a long, multi-generational fight, in which building a common culture is where we need to start.' The necessary conditions for a fairer world system are not yet in place. We need a stronger feeling of global solidarity to develop to create the necessary political will for difficult reforms.

That may not come until, as in 1945, world leaders are forced again to pick up the pieces after a devastating catastrophe. We should hope that it does not take such a course of events and work to reduce that likelihood as much as possible. That, in essence, is what this book is about – thinking through the kind of social movement that can, over time, create the political will for a better world order. But we must not confuse the fact that change is difficult with the idea that the status quo is acceptable. It is not. Hard as it may be to improve the global political system at the present time, a fairer political world order has to be a core component of what responsible globalists are calling for. The unfairness of the current system means that any attempt to win consensus for it is quixotic. Even if it is not in our power today, we need to be clear that we support the creation of a fairer system.

One of the defining features of a nation is that it is a community that aspires to be self-governing. But for many people, even those who are keen supporters of greater global solidarity and cooperation, the idea of a single government for the world is terrifying. Anne-Marie Slaughter claims that 'the size and scope of a [world government] presents an unavoidable and dangerous threat to individual liberty'.[11] She worries about the 'uniformity that would be imposed by a central authority under an imagined and feared world government'.[12] Kwame Anthony Appiah rules out a global state because 'it could easily accumulate uncontrollable power, which it might use to do great harm; it would often be unresponsive to local needs; and it would almost certainly reduce the variety of institutional experimentation from which all of us can learn'.[13]

In my view, these arguments are specious. All governments present a potential threat to individual liberty and can accumulate uncontrollable power and do great harm. There are countless examples throughout history, as well as in today's world, of exactly that. Slaughter recognizes this when she widens her frame of reference to 'the Governance Dilemma: although institutions are essential for human life, they are also dangerous'.[14] But no one is proposing that we should do away with government altogether. As I argued in Chapter 5, the vast majority of powers can and should remain at the nation-state level. That means there is no need for the global system to be unresponsive to local needs, or to end institutional experimentation.

Part of the reason for the refusal to countenance the idea of a global government, I believe, lies in seeing an unworkable 'straw man' of a global government as the only available option. Many of those who have taken on this debate seem to assume that a global government must operate in exactly the same way as current nation-state governments. They then conclude that such an arrangement would not work for the world at large, and therefore that we can have no global government. It is true that implanting the model of a nation-state government on to the world would not work. Even the variation tolerated between states in the US would be far too narrow a straitjacket to impose. But to think about what kind of government a global nation requires, we do not need to assume the replication of existing forms.

Max Weber's timeless definition of a 'state' is that it is a 'human community that (successfully) claims the monopoly of the legitimate use of violence within a given territory'.[15] If a government is 'the group of people with the authority to govern a state',[16] then a government, properly defined, is an institution with a monopoly on legitimate violence. This is the key distinguishing feature between our existing system, where individual countries maintain an entirely independent military strength and defend their right to use it unilaterally, for example in self-defence, and a global government, which would imply that global institutions would be the only actors able to authorize violence legitimately. Of course, countries could have their own armies, in the same way that cities have their own police forces, but they would not be able to use them unilaterally.

Anything more than such a monopoly on legitimate violence is an optional extra, to be considered on its merits. If we were to establish an effective global body, with nation-states as the constituent parts, without whose collective authority any violence was considered illegitimate, we would then have, by definition, a global government. We already have the beginnings of such a system, in the United Nations Security Council. Unfortunately, it is neither just nor effective, nor is it the sole legitimate arbiter in the eyes of most people. Fixing it is exceptionally difficult. But if we could, would that necessarily mean a reduction in individual liberty? Would it necessarily lead to uniformity?

Another important explanation for the view that global government is impossible or undesirable is that many people are quite happy with the government they have. The death and suffering caused by the current system are things that happen to other people in other places. The idea of a global government is especially scary if you currently live in a country like the United States, which is exceptionally powerful and tolerably well governed. In that case, there seems like a lot of risk in shaking things up, especially if that means joining up with other countries with less of a track record of good governance or with a different political system. Americans and Europeans I spoke to most frequently referred to a fear that China's size meant that any global government would mean Chinese domination and an end to democracy.

For people living in badly governed or ungoverned areas, however, the case for a global government is stronger. When countries are invaded or descend into civil war, or minorities are persecuted, those suffering the consequences regularly look to the global system to protect them.[17] They, and compassionate onlookers, ask how the world can allow their suffering to continue. More often than not, they find that there is no reliable system to guarantee their rights. The idea that global government would reduce individual liberty rings hollow to people today who live under regimes where they have no liberty at all.

Given that most people do not live in such dire circumstances and probably have more confidence in their own government than those of other countries, we might expect the vast majority to be totally against the idea of global government. After all, as Lord Malloch-Brown noted, their representatives at the United Nations are nowhere near agreeing on any broadening or deepening of the current system. However, there is far more public support for a strengthening of the global system than the gloomy political climate might suggest. As we saw in Chapter 2, the majority of people in every one of the thirty-three countries surveyed by the International Social Survey Programme, ranging from the USA, Germany and Japan to Mexico, South Africa and India, agreed with the statement 'for certain problems, like environment pollution, international bodies should have the right to enforce solutions'. Another survey, carried out by Com-Res 2017, which targeted 8,000 people in a range of countries which together contain half of the world's population, found that the majority said they want 'a new supranational organization with coercive powers to solve global challenges'.

These are surprising results. Neither of the surveys comes close to demonstrating that world government is achievable. But they do suggest that the majority of people understand that there are global problems which require global solutions, that there are serious weaknesses in the systems we now have, and that some kind of enforcement power would be needed for the system to function perfectly. Environmental degradation has been especially important in this regard. Climate change will not affect every country to the same degree, but it is affecting the rich as well as the poor; well-governed countries as well as lawless areas. There seems much less hope in an isolationist approach to the problem. The public's awareness of this offers hope that steps to strengthen global governance, if well thought through and well explained, have a chance of getting public support in a wide range of countries.

The challenge is in designing a system to which powerful countries are prepared to submit. Champions of the global order like to describe it as a 'rules-based system'. But we have not yet succeeded in convincing the biggest countries to submit to rules. The World Trade Organization is a notable exception – it has developed an effective mechanism for penalizing rule-breakers – precisely the reason Donald Trump's administration is seeking to destroy it.[18]

The US and UK with their invasion of Iraq, Russia with its surreptitious invasion of Ukraine and annexation of Crimea, and China with its activities in the South China Sea have all showed a willingness by permanent members of the UN Security Council to ignore the rules – and the international bodies designed to uphold them – when it suits their perceived national interest. Perhaps the most flagrantly unjust of the international system's 'rules' is that some countries are allowed to have nuclear weapons, while others aren't. I am the last person to advocate the spread of nuclear weapons, but attempts to justify the harsh punishment of countries seeking nuclear arms on the grounds of 'upholding the rules-based system' do not ring true when coming from the only country ever to have used them. Even less so when the US and its allies are known, in one of the worst-kept secrets in geopolitics, to have surreptitiously and illegally allowed Israel to nuclearize its military. The only real justification that can be mustered for this systematic inequality is that 'we are more responsible and respectful of human rights than they are'. Well, perhaps, but other countries can be forgiven for sensing an injustice.

For the most powerful states, which do not much fear the others, any kind of consistent rules can feel like a constraint on their independence. That was Donald Trump's clear message when he spoke at the United Nations General Assembly in September 2018, telling the gathered world leaders that 'America is governed by Americans . . . We reject the ideology of globalism and we embrace the doctrine of patriotism. Around the world, responsible nations must defend against threats to sovereignty not just from global governance but also from other, new forms of coercion and domination.'

History shows us, however, that in the long run, a rules-based system is a better guarantee of protection, even for the mightiest, than the law of the jungle. Mogul India and Imperial China in the early eighteenth century would not have been easy places to make an argument for the submission of rulers to an international order. These two huge empires contained the greater part of the world's population and economy, and each seemed unassailable after generations of unbroken dynastic succession. As late as 1793, the Chinese Emperor Qianlong was content to dismiss the idea of a free trade deal with England because 'there is no need to import the manufactures of outside barbarians in exchange for our own produce'. Far from expecting a rules-based international system, the emperor wrote to King George III as if he were a subject, telling him to 'tremblingly obey and show no negligence'.[19]

However, today's powerful bullies can become tomorrow's aggrieved victims. The following century saw the colonization of India and the humiliation of China through the aggressive 'Opium Wars' waged by Britain and its European allies. Japan and Germany have learned the same lesson more recently. In the first half of the twentieth century both countries went from taking advantage of their relative strength to being on the verge of total destruction as a result of the backlash that ensued. Since then, both have been strong supporters of a multilateral approach to decision-making

The United States, Russia and China are still content to put more trust in their own powers than in any system of rules. In the United States, there is horror in many quarters about the way in which Donald Trump has scorned the UN and the so called 'rules-based system', but underneath the difference in tone there is bipartisan agreement that the US should strive to maintain an exceptional status rather than any notion of equality with other powers. This is reflected, for example, in the United States' withdrawal from the mandatory jurisdiction of the International Court of Justice in 1986 after its covert war against Nicaragua was deemed illegal, and its failure so far to join the International Criminal Court, which was established in 2002. No administration has made a serious attempt to reverse these decisions. Even liberal internationalists such as John Ikenberry, who was fiercely critical of George Bush's 'neo-imperial grand strategy',[20] is content to argue that one of the priorities for strengthening global cooperation is to 'renew American hegemonic authority'.[21] The penny has not yet dropped that attempting hegemony (especially one which is entirely impossible to enforce) stands in contradiction to the goal of creating a rules-based international order.

The perception that freedom is guaranteed only by bullying rights is devilishly hard to break, despite the many examples that reveal its fallacy. The most powerful lesson for me in this regard came with the so-called 'liberation' of my father's country, Iraq. The invasion was code-named Operation Iraqi Freedom and the invading forces, joined by supportive journalists and commentators, were tireless in reminding Iraqis that what they were suffering was a fair price for being 'free'. But freedom and chaos are not the same thing. My cousins, uncles, aunts and friends who lived through that period were all against Saddam Hussein but soon realized that any order is better than no order at all. Freedom to kidnap someone's family is not freedom, because it means that many people are not free to walk the streets. Freedom to inflict violence at will is not freedom, because it means that many people are not free from fear. Freedom to assassinate journalists is not freedom, because it curtails the freedom of the press.

So when Donald Trump says he supports nations being free to do as they choose but in the same breath reminds the world that the United States is spending a record amount on its military – more than $700 billion per year – and goes on to threaten and cajole the countries whose governments he does not like, we should ask ourselves what kind of freedom he is envisioning. True freedom comes through the joint submission to a set of liberal, enforceable rules which allow all parties to pursue their legitimate interests and prevent them from curtailing the freedom of others. That is the kind of global system that can enshrine and protect the nation-state. It requires today's bullies to take an enlightened view of their self-interest.

Taking the long view, there are grounds for optimism. Institutions can evolve to reflect their participants' enlightened, rather than merely their primal, self-interest. We saw in the last chapter how national sentiment and representative government in Western Europe grew slowly in tandem with the higher taxes that states were forced

to raise. The lesson from history is that the growth of national sentiment is the most important enabler for the creation of strong and fair
institutions of government. This basic truth was observed in 1864 by
John Stuart Mill: 'Free institutions are next to impossible in a
country made up of different nationalities. Among a people without
fellow-feeling, especially if they read and speak different languages,
the united public opinion necessary to the working of representative
government cannot exist.'[22]

At first glance, this seems to undermine any attempt at a fair
global system. But Mill does not define nationality in some primor-
dial terms that would permanently separate the peoples of the earth.
Rather, he says that 'a portion of mankind may be said to constitute
a nationality if they are united among themselves by common sym-
pathies'.[23] He goes on to give examples of how different languages,
ethnicities and religions can exist within a single nationality (he cites
Switzerland), and how those sharing a language, ethnicity, religion
and even the same government can feel they are not the same nation
(interestingly, he cites Naples and Sicily, which are now part of the
same Italian nation).

So the nation must come first, representative government second.
What about Mill's own nation – Britain. Or is it England? Scotland
often refers to itself as a nation, but if it is, and Mill was right, then
representative government in the UK is impossible and Scotland
should be independent. If Britain is a nation, it belongs together. This
seems to me the core of the Scottish independence argument – the
question of where nationhood truly lies.

In 2014, the Scots were given the opportunity to answer this question in a referendum. A majority felt that, on balance, they belonged
to a British nation, while a significant minority felt that they did not.
If that seems unsatisfyingly vague, we should not be surprised. Identities are fluid and reside more often within grey areas than absolutes.
Remember that across Europe most people feel that their identity is
equally split between their local region and their nation-state. Nor
should we despair. Britain's evolving governing arrangements have
shown themselves sufficiently flexible to manage the complexity of
British identity. Scotland has both a representative government of its
own and forms part of the government of the UK, neatly matching

Britain's 'just about' nationhood and Scotland's 'almost' nationhood. As identities shift, this arrangement is liable to change again within our lifetimes.

In the same way, the global political system should evolve in line with the development of globalist identity. Until there is much more trust and solidarity between people, it would be premature to move from global governance (an arrangement by which common interests are, in theory, managed cooperatively by entirely independent powers) to global government (whereby global institutions would, in theory, have a monopoly on legitimate violence). The surest way to create the monstrous kind of global government which Slaughter and Appiah fear is for global government to be imposed before the development of the interpersonal solidarity on which it depends. Where states have been built in this way, individual liberty has been sacrificed.

Ethiopia provides a powerful example. The country in its current form was created by the expansion of what was then called Abyssinia under Emperor Menelik II in the late nineteenth century. This programme of conquest brought under the regime's control various peoples, such as the Oromo, whom they had not for centuries, or in some cases ever, ruled. What followed was a century-long attempt to build Ethiopian national identity exclusively from an Abyssinian (Amharic and Tigrean) cultural model, even though the Oromo formed between a third and a half of the Ethiopian population. In the words of sociologist Mekuria Bulcha, 'to be accepted as Ethiopians, the Oromo were expected to completely forget their past, relinquish their culture and language and cease to be Oromo'.[24] During much of the twentieth century, assimilationist policies were imposed by force. The minority of Oromo who were felt to be sufficiently assimilated were referred to as *ye-selettene* ('civilized'), while the non-Amharized majority were called *ye-meeda* ('wild'). The predictable result was a long period of armed struggle. The comparison with today's idea of a 'Western' globalization whereby non-Western people can be 'Westernized' but never fully part of the club is instructive.

In Ethiopia, government policy did not end in the successful elimination of Oromo culture, or its language, which, since the fall of the military regime in 1991, has returned to being a lingua franca in many parts of the country. Now its new prime minister, Abiy Ahmed, who is half Oromo and half Amharic (the first prime minister of Oromo descent), is trying to make up for lost time in building a truly inclusive nation by consent rather than by force.[25] It will not be easy, but it looks more likely to succeed than the twentieth-century policies of repression.

The priority for our times, then, is to ensure that our global governance arrangements match the work-in-progress global nation. Right now, they still lag far behind. Many different answers have been proffered for improving global governance. Perhaps the most influential 'big idea' in recent years has been Anne-Marie Slaughter's 'inter-governmental networks', which she set out in A New World Order in 2005. Slaughter saw a world of 'disaggregated states' where each department in each government had its own network of contacts across the world, among people in other countries with similar roles and working on similar problems. Thus, international networks of judges could work together on harmonizing legal systems and chasing down criminals, networks of finance ministers (for example, through the G20) could coordinate economic policies, and networks of parliamentarians could discuss common approaches to legislation.

These networks are indeed powerful tools for strengthening global governance. Their greatest power, as Slaughter recognizes, is in their ability to create a common culture among bureaucrats in different countries. This is precisely one of the processes of global nation-building in action. But networks are not a silver bullet.

Slaughter's primary example of how they can help is instructive. She argues that inter-governmental networks could have played a more powerful role in helping to rebuild Iraq after the 2003 invasion. Indeed, they could have. But this is to miss the woods for the trees. The invasion of Iraq represents precisely the kind of tragedy that our current, illegitimate world order produces. Networks of judges, trade negotiators or legislators might have helped a little to clear up the mess, although they would not have been able to solve Iraq's most pressing post-war problem: the slide into sectarian conflict. Most importantly, they could have done nothing to prevent the invasion happening in the first place.

The international system, including its official institutions and more informal government networks, has given us a global talking shop of unprecedented scale and utility. This has allowed an incredible amount of progress to be made. Where we have problems in common and agree on the solutions, we can solve them together like never before. We have already halved absolute poverty in less than thirty years. There is a good chance that, in our lifetime, the number of people living on less than $2 per day will drop to zero, that major pandemic disease risks will be averted and mutually beneficial trade deals will continue to be signed.

However, we need to accept the fact that, in some cases, nation-state governments will choose to ignore the network's soft power and will take action that is harmful to the others. No true order can rest on networks of influence alone. In particular, there are four areas in which nation-states can currently harm each other with impunity: by degrading the environment, by operating as tax havens, by refusing to accept refugees and through the unjustified use of military force (including cyber warfare). In each, the global system needs to develop stronger powers for enforcement.

Ultimately, implementing climate-change commitments, following an international consensus on tax and supporting refugees are all questions of economics.[26] The best way to ensure compliance is through applying economic pressure through tariffs and sanctions. That would change a country's calculations in favour of compliance.

It is hard to imagine such a regime coming into force without the support of the three biggest economies in the world – the EU, the US and China. But if those three, under pressure from their citizens, agreed to make compliance on all three issues a condition for trade, the costs for any country deviating would be very high.

That may seem a long way off now. The United States is backtracking on climate change. The EU contains, in Luxembourg, a voting member that is also a tax haven. China has shown little appetite to accept refugees. But over a period of years, progress is possible. The United States contains a strong environmental lobby, which could see its agenda supported by future administrations. Tax avoidance in the EU is becoming a huge issue in all of the largest economies, which could lead them to put sufficient pressure on Luxembourg to change the EU's stance. In China, the government has accepted almost no Syrian refugees, but polling finds that the majority of the population would be happy to accept them.[27] If globalists can make a stronger case for why international enforcement on these issues is necessary to protect their own nation-states, the stalemate can gradually be broken. Perhaps the issue where the most progress is possible most quickly is climate change. If the principle of international enforcement could be established on that, it would open the door to progress on the others.

That leaves the toughest of international dilemmas: how to control the use of force. Again, progress cannot be made without the involvement of the biggest player, which in military terms is, unquestionably, the United States. As time passes and its share of the global economy falls, it must decide whether to attempt to cling on to a fading hegemony or lead the way in crafting a fairer global system. The rising powers have a similar choice – whether to aspire to bullying rights or to push for a bigger role in a system that will guarantee their safety, even when their star is no longer rising. We have certainly not reached the point at which good sense prevails, but we might do so within the lifetimes of many people reading this book. What would a better system look like?

To improve global governance over the use of force we must return to the thorny issue of reforming the United Nations Security Council. Various schemes have been proposed, from adding this or that country, to moving towards a system where each region nominates a representative on a rotating basis.[28] Should a willingness to countenance change re-emerge, the final form that is agreed on will be the result of intense political negotiation. I propose a set of five touchstones to inform this process.

The first is *certainty*. This is the most important attribute of any political system. It is the reason that monarchy, despite its manifest unfairness, has held sway for so many thousands of years in so many places. Simply put, certainty requires that the rules be as fixed as possible and known to all. When rules are changed, the process for changing them should be clear, but this should not happen on a one-off basis. The need for certainty is the best argument for a written constitution, the United States' most important gift to political science.[29]

The current global political system already has a good amount of certainty. There is a written UN Charter. Membership of the Security Council, the rules for selecting non-permanent members and the special privileges for permanent members (notably, their ability to veto any resolution) are known to all. It is imperative that any changes to the system do not reduce the level of certainty. That is why I am sceptical of proposals to add individual countries to permanent membership of the Security Council.

The second touchstone is *flexibility*, another crucial aspect of any political system that intends to reduce the risk of conflict. This is the great downfall of monarchy – when the power balance changes or the rules-based system produces a leader who cannot lead, monarchies tend to be overthrown violently because there is no inbuilt flexibility to allow peaceful change. Flexibility, more than justice, was the main advantage of the parliamentary system that gradually overtook the monarchy as the real power in England (later, Britain) in the early-modern period. Even when King George III went mad, the country continued to function tolerably well.[30] The global order needs flexibility to be built into the system, so that changes in the balance of power do not tend towards violent overthrow of the established order.

Currently, there is almost no flexibility.[31] When the UN was founded, Britain and France represented a huge part of the global economy. Now they are tiny by comparison, but both have kept their permanent seats on the Security Council. India in the same period has gone from being ruled by Britain to being an independent state with an economy larger than that of either Britain or France in terms of purchasing power, but it still has no seat. This inflexibility risks the Security Council being gradually ignored and sliding into irrelevance. This has already happened to some extent, as Shinzō Abe warned in his speech to the General Assembly in 2018.[32]

One way of achieving flexibility without sacrificing certainty is by using weighted voting and giving countries a share of decision-making power that reflects their population, the size of their economy and their contribution to foreign aid. Factoring in population ensures that the system is representative; adding the economy ensures that the system recognizes the reality of power; and foreign aid ensures that countries have to pay to play, rather than free-riding on the global system. As discussed in Chapter 5, I propose that foreign aid should be calculated as a share of the wealth tax raised on the assets of millionaires. Any additional contributions would not lead to more voting power, thereby preventing countries from buying undue influence.

The third touchstone is *selective inclusiveness*. Having established weighted voting, some important decisions could be taken by a larger set of countries. Currently, the all-important issues of war and peace are reserved for the fifteen-member Security Council. The vast majority of countries are not consulted. On the other hand, the General Assembly has one vote for each member, even though that includes behemoths such as China and minnows like Guam. That means that its resolutions do not reflect the people or the power structure of the world. In acknowledgement of that fact, they have never had more than advisory status. If the General Assembly's resolutions had more authority, the one-state-one-vote system would incentivize nation-states to disintegrate – any region would have far more power as an independent country with its own vote than as part of a bigger block. Such a strong systematic incentive for partitioning countries would doubtless instigate a whole range of conflicts.

However, with weighted voting, the General Assembly could make much more meaningful and enforceable decisions with a far greater degree of legitimacy, while maintaining the respect for Realpolitik that is necessary for any decision to be upheld. No country could claim it had no voice in the major decisions. But its voice would, quite reasonably, be tempered by its size and power.

That does not mean that every decision would need to be made by the votes of nearly 200 countries. As Ian Goldin, a professor of Globalization and Development at Oxford University, has forcefully argued, the complexities of reaching agreements with dozens of stakeholders mean that on an issue-by-issue basis only the relevant countries need to be engaged.[33] Malloch-Brown argues for the importance of a small group of countries playing the role of the Security Council, because of the need for detailed ongoing scrutiny and decision-making. For example, the mandate in Libya, where use of force to protect civilians was authorized by the Security Council in 2011, needs to be renewed every three months. That would be impracticable with too large a group.

However, the biggest decisions, such as whether to authorize the use of force in the first place, could and should be collective global decisions. The intentional destruction of human life on a large scale, through bombing, invasion or any other method, is too important, too morally problematic, has too many global repercussions and is too open to abuse to be delegated to the committee level. In my view, legitimacy requires global consent.

The fourth touchstone is *supermajority*. In any system of voting, the level of consensus necessary for decision-making has far-reaching implications. In the United States, regular legislation requires a simple majority (i.e. above 50 per cent) in Congress, but amendments to the constitution require a supermajority (i.e. two thirds of both houses of Congress), or a constitutional convention called by two thirds of state legislatures. In the UK, a simple majority is sufficient for any decision. This allows governments to implement their agenda highly effectively but can produce challenges of legitimacy, such as when the constitutionally crucial vote to leave the EU was carried by a tiny majority. Meanwhile, the EU itself in recent years has moved from a system where every country had a veto on every issue, which had blocked progress in many areas, to one where in some decisions a supermajority is sufficient.[34] In all of these and every other vote-based system, important implications are carried by the system chosen. In general, the higher the bar for consensus (at the extreme, giving every member a veto), the greater the legitimacy of any decision taken, while a lower bar (such as requiring only a simple majority), increases effectiveness – the ability for decisions to be made.

In the Security Council as it stands some countries have a veto and others do not. This system is neither legitimate, as it is viewed by most countries as unfair, nor is it effective, as the veto is regularly used to block action. In my view, the UN should operate on the principle of supermajority, with a high bar for consensus, set, say at 80 per cent of weighted votes. That would be enough to ensure that no one country, even China or the US, could unilaterally block action. But one of them with a few allies, or a bigger collection of smaller countries, could do so. Reflecting the practical difficulties of imposing decisions in the teeth of the most powerful countries, this could be done only when they were completely isolated. That would force even the geopolitical bullies to ensure they cultivated some alliances. Importantly, every country would be treated the same, in line with its population and economic size. It would, of course, be nice if total legitimacy could be achieved for decisions by giving every country a veto, but that would be to guarantee that no enforcement against offenders was ever possible. Widening the inclusivity of global decision-making requires us to limit the threshold for consensus.

Of course, in a divided world, this system of supermajority with weighted voting would not unblock action on every issue. However, it would be unlikely to reduce the system's effectiveness (i.e. the ability to take decisions) from its current low level, while massively increasing its legitimacy. Where decisions were taken, the likelihood that the world would be prepared to enforce them would be much higher.

The fifth touchstone is *respect for difference*. In any political system, this is what separates democracy from mob role. Even if most people do not behave like me, I should be able to carry on being different as long as I am causing no harm. In the same way, even with a supermajority of 80 per cent, it is not acceptable for the world to gang up on Kenya, Ecuador, Mongolia or any other nation-state and tell them how to manage their affairs. It is this principle above all that can defend against the creation of a monolithic world government that insists on uniformity.

Happily, respect for difference already exists in the global system and is unlikely to be challenged any time soon. Even with the greater level of legitimacy created by the principles outlined above, enforcement will continue to be highly politically risky, operationally difficult and costly. So there is no reason to believe that a more legitimate global system would suddenly lead to obligatory uniformity. On the contrary, an inclusive system would allow countries to better resist any pressures to conform. So long as their publics ask them to, governments will jealously guard their right to pursue their own path and will vote accordingly.

Respect for difference implies that the global system should be allowed to engage only in three areas. Where all countries are agreed, they can mandate the global system to play a role. A good example of this is the Global Goals, which were agreed by all UN member states in 2015 and are now a collective project for all of them. Furthermore, a single country, or subset of countries, can mandate the global system to play a role in coordinating or managing some part of their affairs, so long as this does not interfere with the countries not party to the agreement. A good example of this is the International Commission against Impunity in Guatemala, a UN agency that was set up at Guatemala's invitation in 2007, when the country realized that it needed outside help to deal with rampant corruption. Guatemala alone can, and should, decide whether the commission continues to work in their country.[35]

Then there are the rare cases of enforcement. Right now, the Security Council is entitled to authorize the use of sanctions and, ultimately, military force in three different scenarios. Firstly, according to Chapter VII of the UN Charter, to resist 'threats to the peace, breaches of the peace and acts of aggression', in other words, preventing international conflict. Secondly, according to Chapter XIV of the UN Charter, if countries are in breach of their international obligations according to the judgement of the International Court of Justice, the Security Council can 'decide upon measures to be taken to give effect to the judgement'. Thirdly, the Security Council can interfere in a country's internal affairs if that country is in breach of its responsibility to protect its own citizens from 'genocide, war crimes, ethnic cleansing or crimes against humanity'. This 'responsibility to protect', and the international community's responsibility to step in when it is not met, was agreed by every member of the United Nations in 2005, as a result of the World Summit held that year.[36]

In other words, the Security Council already has a mandate to carry out all the enforcement tasks I have argued for, not only regarding military force, but also to impose economic sanctions on countries breaking treaty obligations, such as on climate change, refugees and tax.[37] Nothing more needs to be added to these rights and responsibilities for global enforcement. Some countries will continue to be run by military dictatorships. That should be allowed – the global system does not have the legitimacy or the right to determine that a country's system of government is the wrong one. Some court systems or police forces will continue to perform poorly. The global system should offer technical support but not seek to enforce a change.

These, then, are the five touchstones that I commend to globalists as we seek to put global governance reform back on the political agenda: certainty, flexibility, selective inclusiveness, supermajority and respect for difference. This is not a proposal for global government. The UN process would not aggregate to itself the sole legitimacy in authorizing the use of force, because countries would retain the right to defend themselves unilaterally when attacked. The use of force domestically against offenders would continue to be legitimate without authorization by the UN system.

One can imagine over the long term moving to a system whereby a reformed UN had so much efficacy, legitimacy and popularity that it was able to rapidly authorize self-defence when required. Each country might have to receive periodic approval for its system for the internal use of force against offenders or threats to the peace. That would be a truly global government. For now, applying the five principles suggested above would take the world far closer to being a 'parliament of man', as Tennyson envisioned so long ago.

Conclusion: A Choice of Paths

> STRANGER: *Where shall we discover the path of the States-*
> *man? [. . .]*
> SOCRATES: *To find the path is your business, Stranger,*
> *and not mine.*
>   Plato, *Statesman*, fourth century BC

The gradual emergence of a global nation is possible. In fact, it is already happening, not just in business-class lounges and around the conference-room tables of the United Nations and the World Bank, but in the homes and the minds of billions of people spread across every country. Globalist identity remains a fragile sentiment. It competes with a narrower nationalism which proclaims that each person's concern – at the very most – is the advancement of their nation-state. And it goes against yet narrower views: only my ethnic group, only my class, only my family deserve my help. But history has shown us that the idea of many different communities, each with their own history and identity, belonging to a single, indivisible nation, can surge within a few decades, transforming identity, politics and society in its wake.

This did not mean the end of allegiances to family, region, class or religion. It simply meant that, in the final calculation, the good of the nation cannot be sacrificed at their altar. This new bond was sometimes used for hostile and unjust ends. Yet it has only been when a strong national sentiment is evident that humans have shown an ability to live in democracies, under the rule of law, with a great part of their collective income channelled towards projects designed to achieve the common good. This has allowed us to tackle many of the collective problems that exist within the borders of nation-states. To solve our many global challenges, that myth of common nationhood should be extended much further.

The challenge is to win over those who are not yet convinced. When nations have been imposed from above on an unwilling public, they have always either failed, or succeeded at far too great a cost. Winning over the anti-globalists should not be done by pandering to one group or another but by looking hard at the injustices that the global system currently embodies and working to fix them. If we can start talking about ourselves as humans in a truly inclusive way; if we can turn the dry document of the UN's Global Goals into a visceral mission for humanity and channel our urge to fight 'the other' into a fight against climate change, disease and poverty; if we can resist any urge to undermine nation-states, democratic decision-making and the right of populations to control the pace of change of their communities; if we can use global cooperation to ensure that all wealth is identified and taxed; if we can push the United Nations towards being a more legitimate and effective body; then, I believe, despite inevitable reverses along the way, a stronger human solidarity is possible.

While prediction is futile, it is possible to identify various paradigms for how the global nation might evolve, based on the experience of nation-building projects in the past. I will conclude by outlining three scenarios worth considering. Perhaps none of these will come to pass. Perhaps it will be a combination of them all. Either way, they may provide a helpful framework as we feel our way into the future.

The first scenario is that of Arab nationalism. In a short amount of time, it achieved its goal of uniting hundreds of millions of people in the belief that they were all 'Arabs' and that this was a meaningful social and political identity requiring a degree of solidarity and common action. That was a remarkable achievement. When Arab nationalism took off as a mass movement less than a century ago, almost no Moroccans had ever visited Iraq, nor Egyptians met a Yemeni. On the rare occasions when they did, they struggled very hard to understand each other, despite speaking variants of what Arab nationalists insisted was a single language. Until the twentieth century, the word 'Arab' meant a desert dweller; it indicated of a way of life, not an ethnicity. People in the cities often spoke Arabic, the language of the desert, which was also the language of the Quran. But that did not lead them to consider themselves 'Arabs'.

In any case, the urban classes were often natively bilingual, speaking Turkish if, like my great-grandparents, they lived in the Ottoman lands, or French and Amaziq if they came from the Maghreb. It therefore took an act of imagination and creative genealogy to determine that this new identity – 'Arabness' – applied to them. My father's family, whose earliest known ancestor was a seventeenth-century Ottoman general, a suspiciously Turkish occupation, hurriedly found documents demonstrating that we had in fact migrated to northern Iraq from Yemen and had good, Arab roots in the Shureifat tribe.

Arab nationalism had blistering success in reordering the identity of a great part of the Middle East and North Africa. The result is a touching social bond between people over a vast region. Despite being born in Britain with just one Arab parent, when I travel to any country from Morocco to Oman, this ancestry and my imperfect Arabic are enough to instantly convince the local population that, in some meaningful way, I am 'one of them'.

However, as a political project, Arab nationalism utterly failed. The first failure was that it was not sufficiently inclusive. Kurds and Amaziq, the latter of whom form a majority in several 'Arab' countries, did not see themselves in the new-found ethnonym. Shi'a, while agreeing that they were Arabs, often opposed the political project because it would make their religious group a minority in what they saw, often rightly, as an attempt to remake a Sunni caliphate.

The second failure was one of implementation. Shepherding a large number of different government systems, with all their privileges, interests and constituencies, into a single, larger system is no easy task. The European Union has learned that a gradual approach can be frustrating, but it has not (yet) collapsed. Arab unification was attempted on the quick. In 1958, Syria and Egypt unified as the United Arab Republic. Egypt's President Gamal Abdel Nasser felt rushed into the decision. Due thought had not been given as to how to manage the personalities, the power dynamics and the distribution of roles. Within three years, the project had failed. Meanwhile,

Iraq, Egypt's arch-rival at the time, attempted its own unification project by combining with Jordan in 1958 to form the United Hashemite Kingdom. By the end of the year a popular coup in Baghdad had ended that scheme too. The Arab League, an older organization than the European Union, has made precious little progress over the decades in bridging the political differences between its members. Today, all that remains of Arab nationalism is a feeling of social solidarity. War, trade barriers and immigration controls are more prevalent than anywhere else on earth. With political cooperation limited, climate change is rendering vast areas uninhabitable.

To my mind, this is a highly realistic scenario for the global nation. Even if migration is radically reduced, many of the forces that are encouraging people to prioritize a common human identity will likely remain in place. Internet access is increasingly available at higher bandwidths. The spread of education and the priority put in every country on learning English is creating the possibility for content to be shared and understood in every town and village. But the continued insistence that the emerging global mainstream culture is inherently 'Western' is likely to leave large minorities, especially those in political conflict with the US and her allies, seeing no place for themselves within it. Faced with the United States jealously guarding the remains of its hegemony, rising powers are likely to carve out spheres of influence of their own. As a result, politicians may well waste the opportunity to make the United Nations a more flexible, legitimate body that can slowly achieve greater political unity. We may end up, like most Arabs, with the strong sense that we belong to a single nation but little progress to show for it.

The second scenario is Chinese nationalism. On its own terms, this has been a resounding success. As Wang Hui notes, 'China is the only empire which existed before the 19th century, which maintained its territory and population in a 21st-century "nation-state". All the others disintegrated in the face of nationalist separatist movements.'[1] China was even able, after the political disruption and civil war that marked the first half of the twentieth century, to reincorporate the empire's lost territories of Tibet and Xinjiang, where the majority populations had very different cultural identities and political histories. Both provinces are home to secessionist movements, but neither has been able to pose a serious challenge to Beijing's authority.

Perhaps more remarkable than China's ability to regain and hold on to peripheral regions, is the high degree of solidarity across its vast eastern heartland. The unity of the Han as 'a single people' is just as imaginary as the differences that distinguish Portuguese, Spaniards, French, Italians and Romanians, whose Latin-derived languages are just as mutually incomprehensible as the dialects of Chinese. But no independent ethnicity-based political identity has developed among Cantonese speakers, despite having a geographical homeland and a distinguishing language. Indeed, Sun Yat-Sen, one of the most prominent founders of Chinese nationalism, was Cantonese. Even in Hong Kong, the political movement for more autonomy from Beijing has not sought to distinguish the Cantonese people, or Hong Kong itself, as a separate nation. Taiwan is of course administered separately, but its political history is as a rival Chinese government, not an attempt to split off. Against all odds, even there the myth of an indivisible Chinese nation is maintained.

So, as a project to maintain the unity of the ancient Chinese Empire, while transitioning to the idea of the sovereignty of the people (clearly articulated in the formula 'People's Republic'), Chinese nationalism has achieved its aims. After unleashing market forces and opening up to international trade, it has also lifted hundreds of millions of people out of poverty.

For all that, Chinese nationalism is another cautionary tale. Rather than an assertion of belonging that demands no more than a basic solidarity, the government has interpreted nationhood as requiring absolute loyalty to a particular party and a particular political vision. Disagreement and debate are conflated with disorder. Any desire for autonomy is squashed.

The authoritarian nature of Chinese nationalism is perhaps most keenly felt in the regions where that national identity is in question – Tibet and Xinjiang. There, a grand project is underway to remake identity through both migration (the inflow of ethnic Han people to change the demographic balance) and acculturation (up to 1 million Muslim Uyghurs at the time of writing were reported to be detained in 're-education camps').[2]

Indeed, the Chinese state requires conformity and severely restricts the freedom of all its citizens, whatever their ethnicity. The most frightening recent development in this regard is probably the emerging Social Credit System, which is compulsory from 2020. The system ranks every citizen and business based on their trustworthiness, through analysis of a vast trove of electronic data gathered by the state. There are rewards for 'honest and trustworthy citizens' and punishments for offenders. In the American and European media the system has been treated as a shocking breach of freedom akin to Big Brother in George Orwell's *Nineteen Eighty-Four*, or the strikingly prescient 'Nosedive' episode of British dystopian sci-fi series *Black Mirror*.[3] Naturally, the official Chinese version of the story is more positive, stressing the benefits that good scores bring to citizens (lower bus fares) and businesses (easier credit).[4] But even in the official narrative, there is nothing to suggest that the system will not be used to shape society in the government's image and suppress any hint of dissent.

No wonder so many people's nightmare of a more unified world looks something like the Chinese state writ large. Its ability to control 1.4 billion people in this way offers a warning to globalists. In my view, this scenario cannot be ruled out and must be defended against. But it remains an unlikely outcome for humanity at large.

The Chinese Han community's impressive social solidarity is a product of thousands of years under a single state, albeit with some intermissions.[5] The Han, in turn, form an overwhelming majority among Chinese people.[6] That has allowed a single self-identifying group to establish itself and for its leaders to demand a high degree of uniformity. The world at large is far more complex. No self-identifying group within it forms more than a small minority. Even after invading comparatively small and weak countries like Iraq and Afghanistan, the most powerful country on earth has shown itself unable to exert political control effectively. The idea of a central global government's interference in the daily lives of people is farfetched. Any form of unity, if it is ever achieved, is likely to be a compromise agreement between various different centres of power. That means it is likely to remain a highly diverse world.

For the people who are least well served by the current global order, who reside in ungoverned, war-torn or desperately poor places, a world run like the Chinese state would be a great improvement. But for many of us, it would mean an unacceptable loss of liberty. Its likelihood will depend not only on geopolitics but also on the development of the data and arms industries, and therefore the ability of governments to extend control over their citizens in the way China is attempting. In the medieval world of knights in heavy armour fighting on horseback, few people could afford to be effective fighters, meaning that a small number of people could control a vast area with little need for representative government. In the world of easily affordable rifles, popular uprisings could cause revolutions and governments had to listen to the people. Even with the emergence of drones and the other accoutrements of modern warfare, it is hard to extend an empire over angry citizens with Kalashnikovs. So far, in most countries, the use of technology has been as much a force for popular mobilization as for government control. In the future, this balance could shift again.

All this stresses the need to protect and enhance the democratic systems that exist today and to refuse any attempt to undermine them, whether in service of global unity or any other goal. If the democratic traditions, already long-standing in some countries, while newly established in others, hold fast in the coming decades, a unifying world can avoid becoming an authoritarian superstate.

The third scenario is post-partition India. There are some ways in which India might be considered a less successful national project than China. Certainly, its economy has not grown as fast in recent decades. Its national solidarity is also less secure. India was born in a bloody partition, through which the Muslim-majority states in the north-east and north-west split off to form Pakistan, which later split again into Pakistan and Bangladesh. It is estimated that nearly a million people died, and ethnic cleansing on both sides forced tens of millions to start new lives in a strange place with no assets save for what they were carrying. But since then India has been an improbable success. The Muslims who did not leave to join Pakistan represent 20 per cent of the population. No one language has a native majority. For almost all of its known history, India has not been governed as a single state. And yet, slowly, falteringly, an Indian national identity has emerged. Just as improbably, democracy has prevailed as the unchallenged governing system.

India after partition is a very possible model for the emergence of a global nation. That is not to flatter India, nor to be overly bullish about the future of global politics. Like the rest of the world, India contains some very rich people but many more who are desperately poor. There is significant prejudice based on religion. Atrocities have been carried out. Maoist insurgents have terrorized large areas for much of India's recent history. The class system, ingrained through inherited 'castes', constrains social mobility. Indians have sufficient national solidarity to sustain a central government but not enough to persuade them to pay more than 11 per cent of their GDP in taxes to the central government (a further 7 per cent is collected by states).[7]

And yet, despite all this, it has become a nation. This has not solved all of India's problems, far from it. But it is hard to imagine that it would be better off as a collection of smaller, potentially warring states. The ongoing hostility between India and Pakistan, which has lasted since their formation and is now a nuclear stand-off, with borders closed to people and goods, articulates that point well enough.

India's nationhood provides the opportunity to put the resources, the willpower and the coordination required into achieving ambitious goals. To give just one example, the central government has been working since 1986 to ensure full access to sanitation services for its vast population. Nowadays, 92 per cent of households are reported to have access to toilets, up from just 37 per cent in 2012. The target of 100 per cent looks likely to be reached in 2019. The programme has not been without its problems and its critics, but such progress would be unimaginable without the kind of coordination that a unified nation can bring.

Like the world at large, India stands at a crossroads. The paths before it lead either to inclusiveness and the entrenchment of pluralistic democracy or to a populist, majoritarian politics that seeks to bully the minority into submission. Founded by leaders who worked tirelessly to insist that all of India's religious groups truly belonged, India is now governed by a party that has always been clear that only Hindus represent the true Indian culture.

The Indians I interviewed for this book told me that the country is increasingly asking itself which model of development it should follow. Should it continue with the liberal democratic model of the United States, which has underpinned many of the most successful economies on earth but is now challenged by a crisis of self-confidence? Or should it turn towards a more authoritarian Chinese model, which has produced the biggest, most sustained economic growth spurt in living memory but is not a system that most humans say they want to live under? Wrapped up in that decision is the treatment of minorities, the level of personal freedom and, ultimately, the type of national identity that emerges.

If we are lucky, India will continue in its faltering path towards a broader idea of the nation and the ambition to improve the lives of all its people. If we are even luckier, humanity will turn out much like India has to date: imperfect but somehow aware of its common past and its destiny; each language, each religion and each state proud of its unique social bond but with just about enough solidarity between them all to allow us to tackle our biggest challenges.

Acknowledgements

This book would not have been possible without the help and patience of many people. Most of all, Anna Jewsbury, the love of my life, for whom the year that her husband was writing his first book was also the first year in the life of our son, Rafi. Without her support and encouragement, I would never have dreamed of taking on this project. The other person without whom this book would not exist is my dear friend Will Hammond, who saw in my first scrappy notes the kernel of an idea worth publishing and gave me access to the full range of his remarkable contact list.

Huge thanks are due to my agent Chris Wellbelove of Aitken Alexander, who showed me how to turn an idea into a proposal and suggested a restructuring that turned this from a dusty academic tome into a far more relevant and readable book. Equally huge thanks to this book's editor, Casiana Ionita, who was a source of many improvements and refinements and, even more importantly, of encouragement. Invariably, I entered our meetings convinced that the project was doomed and left feeling ready to conquer the world.

This book is not connected to my work at the Bill & Melinda Gates Foundation and is a personal project. But I do want to thank my colleagues for their support. In particular, Joe Cerrell has been the best line-manager anyone could ask for – a fount of advice, positivity and encouragement. Gabriella Stern, Carolyn Esser and Drew Porter took time out of their busy schedules to offer advice and help me ensure no conflicts with the foundation's work.

If I am more optimistic about the world than most, a large part of that stems from the experience of getting to know Bill and Melinda Gates, whose straightforward dedication to positive change stands as an unspoken rebuke to any cynic who thinks that progress is not possible. I will always be grateful to them, and the foundation, for giving me the privilege of sitting in an organization driven by the idea that 'all lives have equal value'.

I also want to thank the many people who agreed to talk to me, on and off the record, for my research. They include Bill Gates, Riz Ahmed, Richard Curtis, Anthony Kwame Appiah, Yanis Varoufakis, Sir Nick Clegg, Paul Collier, David Goodhart, Lord Mark Malloch-Brown, Sara Elamine, Lynn Taliento, Mihoko Kashiwakura, Hari Menon, Harris Mylonas, Lady Eleanor Shawcross Wolfson, Ameet Gill, Renad Mansour, Alex Hartley, Ambassador Feisal Istrabadi, Sabrina Mahfouz and Michelle Hutchinson, as well as others who asked not to be mentioned here.

A smaller number of close friends with relevant expertise spent time picking through some or all of the evolving manuscript, and to them I am extremely grateful. They made the sacrifice of wading through a far inferior version of this book, but their input was a vital help. They include my dear brother, Salem Al-Damluji, Alexander Woollcombe, Mike Martin, Tom Dougherty, Claudio Sopranzetti, Alex Fattal and Alice Fordham.

I owe a great deal to all of the people mentioned above, and others who are not named. However, any mistakes or omissions are my own.

Notes

1. From 'Oh my blamer'(يا لائمي) (date unspecified) in *The Complete Arabic Works of Gibran Khalil Gibran* (المجموعة الكاملة لمؤلفات جبران خليل جبران العربية), (2014). My translation from the Arabic.

INTRODUCTION

1. Paul Ignotus, *Hungary* (London: Benn, 1972), p. 44.
2. For a classic account of the simultaneous existence of many group identities in the same person, see Amartya Sen, *Identity and Violence: The Illusion of Destiny* (London: Allen Lane, 2006), where he unpicks 'the odd presumption that . . . human beings [are] members of exactly one group'.
3. For a discussion of the intimate link between industrial society and the development of nationalism, see Ernest Gellner's seminal work *Nations and Nationalism* (Oxford: Blackwell, 1983).
4. See, for example, Kwame Anthony Appiah, *Cosmopolitanism: Ethics in a World of Strangers* (London: Allen Lane: 2006).
5. For a discussion of the evolutionary basis of group identity and violence, see Mike Martin, *Why We Fight* (London: Hurst & Company, 2018).
6. It should be noted that many people who are hostile to foreign aid vastly overestimate how much of the government budget it represents. For example, in the US, the average estimate is that foreign aid is 25 per cent of the budget. Only 5 per cent of respondents know that it is in fact less than 1 per cent. https://www.kff.org/global-health-policy/poll-finding/data-note-americans-views-on-the-u-s-role-in-global-health/.
7. For costs of German reunification, see '*Das Land der zwei Billionen*' in *Welt am Sonntag,* 4 May 2014; https://www.welt.de/print/wams/politik/article127589555/Das-Land-der-zwei-Billionen.html.

8. Germany did, however, repay the profits it had made from Greek debt; https://www.ft.com/content/9b3d38a2-7574-11e8-aa31-31da4279a601.
9. For historical estimates of world population, see: http://www.worldometers.info/world-population/world-population-by-year/.
10. International Social Survey Programme, 2003.
11. Johann Kaspar Riesbeck, *Briefe eines reisenden Franzosen über Deutschland* (Zurich, 1783), ed. Wolfgang Gerlach (Frankfurt am Main, 1967), pp. 330–36.

GLOBALISTS AND NATIONALISTS

1. Some of the most authoritative studies to define nationalism and trace its development include: Benedict Anderson, *Imagined Communities: Reflections on the Origin and Spread of Nationalism* (London: Verso, 1983), Ernest Gellner, *Nations and Nationalism* (Oxford: Blackwell, 1983), Eric Hobsbawm, *Nations and Nationalism since 1780: Programme, Myth, Reality* (Cambridge: Cambridge University Press, 1990), Elie Kedourie, *Nationalism* (Oxford: Blackwell, 4th edn, 1993) and Anthony D. Smith, *Nations and Nationalism in a Global Era* (Cambridge: Polity, 1995).
2. Prior to the French Revolution, the term 'nation' had various nebulous meanings, which ranged from geographic to ethnic to linguistic but did not express the political idea of a natural grouping of humanity holding inherent sovereignty and a claim to self-government (Elie Kedourie, *Nationalism* (Oxford: Blackwell, 4th edn, 1993), pp. 4–7).
3. Jules Michelet, *Histoire de la Révolution française*, cited in Annie Crépin, '*Le Mythe de Valmy*' in *Révolution et république: L'Exception française*, ed. Michel Vovelle (Paris: Éditions Kimé, 1994), p. 470.
4. William Doyle, *The Oxford History of the French Revolution* (Oxford: Oxford University Press, 2002), p. 193.
5. Quoted from Elie Kedourie, op. cit., p. 101.
6. Kant, *Metaphysics of Morals Vigilantius*, XXVII.2.1, 673–4, quoted by Pauline Kleingeld in 'Kant's Cosmopolitan Patriotism', *Kant Studien*, 94 (3), pp. 299–316 (2003).
7. International Social Survey Programme, 2013. The data are discussed in more detail on pages 22–6.
8. Theresa May, Keynote speech to the Conservative Party Conference, 5 October 2016. Full text available at: https://www.independent.co.uk/news/uk/politics/theresa-may-speech-tory-conference-2016-in-full-transcript-a7346171.html.

9. Robert Putnam, '*E Pluribus Unum:* Diversity and Community in the Twenty-first Century', (The 2006 Johan Skytte Prize Lecture)' in *Scandinavian Political Studies* (2006).

10. Mary Beard, *SPQR: A History of Ancient Rome* (London: Profile, 2015).

11. Christine Isom-Verhaaren, 'Constructing Ottoman Identity in the Reigns of Mehmed II and Bayezid II', *Journal of the Ottoman and Turkish Studies Association* (2014).

12. Rarely until the dawn of industrialization did any of these identities claim the right to self-government. Only when nationalism spread to the empire's hub in western Turkey in the late nineteenth century did the Ottoman elite try to create an Ottoman nation, turning the empire's peoples into 'Ottoman citizens'. But by then other competing nationalisms – Turkish, Greek, Armenian, and so on – had the upper hand.

13. It is worth noting that, even in Russia, the elite had once been ethnically distinct Scandinavians – the term *Rus* meaning 'Viking' – although they were culturally integrated into their Slavic domains by the early modern period. Nevertheless, Muscovite princes continued to celebrate their Germanic ancestry until the emergence of nationalist sentiments persuaded them to identify themselves as ethnically identical to the people they ruled. In the nineteenth century, to reinforce this ethnic U-turn, new, wholly fictitious etymologies were invented for the word *Rus*. (See Serhii Plokhi, *Lost Kingdom: The Quest for Empire and the Making of the Russian Nation* (New York: Basic Books, 2017).

14. Hagen Schulze, *The Course of German Nationalism: From Frederick the Great until Bismarck, 1763–1867* (Cambridge: Cambridge University Press, 1991), p. 59.

15. Between the 1920s and the 1950s, secondary-school enrolment in Egypt rose from 5,000 to 120,000, and in Iraq from just 229 to 74,000. Adeed Dawisha, *Arab Nationalism in the Twentieth Century: From Triumph to Despair* (Princeton: Princeton University Press, 2003), pp. 81 & 125.

16. Sandra Davie, 'Singapore Maths Inspires UK Educators', *Strait Times*, 4 April 2017.

17. The bitter argument over whether Nice belonged to France or Italy was a case in point. Nice was the birthplace of Giuseppe Garibaldi, hero of Italian nationalism, and its native language was neither French nor Italian but something in between. The decision to incorporate it into France in 1860 was nothing more than a political concession

made to the French Emperor Napoleon III to secure his acceptance of the creation of a unified Italy.

18. Denis Mack Smith, *Mazzini* (New Haven/London: Yale University Press, 1994).

19. Hobsbawm, op. cit., 60ff.

20. A case in point is provided by the European Union, where English is expected to continue as the main working language even after Britain's exit. English will be the first language of only a tiny fraction of European bureaucrats but will remain the only language understood by almost all.

21. 'Total of 9.4 million students to attend 2017 Gaokao in China', Xinhua News Agency, 6 June 2017.

22. Nicholas Ostler, *The Last Lingua Franca: English until the Return of Babel* (New York: Walker & Co., 2010).

23. According to Lucy Riall, in *Garibaldi: Invention of a Hero* (New Haven/London: Yale University Press, 2007), p. 139, in the 1850s the most widely read newspaper in Piedmont, the hub of both journalism and nationalist sentiment, was the pro-unification *Gazzetta del Popolo,* with no more than 10,000 subscribers. Meanwhile, the population of Italy was approximately 25 million, according to Idamaria Fusco in her 2011 article 'The Unification of Italy, Population, Territorial Imbalances: Some Data and Remarks on Southern Italian Population in the Italian Context (1760–1880)'.

24. For 2018 figures, see Ben Gilbert, 'YouTube Now Has over 1.8 Billion Users Every Month, within Spitting Distance of Facebook's 2 Billion', *Business Insider UK*, 4 May 2018 (accessed September 2018 at: http://uk.businessinsider.com/youtube-user-statistics-2018-5). For 2013 figures, see 'YouTube Stats: Site Has 1 Billion Active Users Each Month', *Huffington Post*, 21 March 2013 (accessed September 2018 at: https://www.huffingtonpost.com/2013/03/21/youtube-stats_n_2922543.html?guccounter=1).

25. In September 2017 the most ever views for a YouTube video was 3.7 billion, for the video of a song called 'Despacito' by Puerto Rican singer Luis Fonsi. It had reached its first billion views in just ninety-seven days.

26. For 2018, see: https://www.fifa.com/worldcup/news/more-than-half-the-world-watched-record-breaking-2018-world-cup. For 2006, see https://www.independent.co.uk/sport/football/news-and-comment/why-fifas-claim-of-one-billion-tv-viewers-was-a-quarter-right-5332287.html.

27. The term, and the theory, were popularized by Cass Sunstein in *Echo Chambers: Bush v. Gore: Impeachment and Beyond* (Princeton: Princeton University Press, 2001).

28. A 2018 study of the online behaviour of 2,000 Britons found that only 8 per cent lived in a media echo-chamber (Elizabeth Dubois, 'The Echo Chamber is Overstated: The Moderating Effect of Political Interest and Diverse Media', in *Information, Communication and Society*, 2018). A survey of American voters in the lead-up to the 2016 presidential election found that the majority of people are members of social networks with a mix of different political views (Maeve Duggan and Aaron Smith, 'The Political Environment on Social Media', published by Pew Research Center, 25 October 2016 (accessed September 2018 at: http://assets.pewresearch.org/wp-content/uploads/sites/14/2016/10/24160747/PI_2016.10.25_Politics-and-Social-Media_FINAL.pdf). Another 2016 study, which looked at the browsing histories of 50,000 US-based internet users, found that social-media usage was 'associated with an increase in an individual's exposure to material from his or her less preferred side of the political spectrum' (Seth Flaxman et al., 'Filter Bubbles, Echo Chambers and Online News Consumption', in *Public Opinion Quarterly*, 2016). While less research has been done on this phenomenon in other parts of the world, there is no reason to expect that the 'echo chamber' claim has any more truth to it anywhere else.
29. Anderson, op. cit.
30. Association of Train Operating Countries (ATOC), 'The Billion Passenger Railway: Lessons from the Past: Prospects for the Future' (2008).
31. Chinese Ministry of Education data (Chinese source: http://www.moe.gov.cn/jyb_xwfb/xw_fbh/moe_2069/xwfbh_2017n/xwfb_170301/170301_sjtj/201703/t20170301_297676.html).
32. Yearbook of International Organizations.
33. Bob Reinalda, *Routledge History of International Organizations* (London: Routledge, 2009), pp. 52–6.
34. Eref Ertürk, 'Intergovernmental Organizations (IGOs) and Their Roles and Activities in Security, Health, and Environment', *Journal of International Social Research*, vol. 8, issue 37, April 2015.
35. Data on staff numbers of international organizations is hard to come by. The United Nations and its agencies in 2012 had around 90,000 staff, according to the UN website (https://www.unsceb.org/content/total-staff-organization), but this represents just a fraction of those employed to carry out the UN's work. Temporary staff, consultants, contractors and grantees should rightly be considered part of the same organizational culture. The UN's 2016 budget was $48.8 billion (this includes all UN agencies except the World Bank and the IMF). Applying some reasonable assumptions gives us a range for

those who could be considered 'UN people' of between 500,000 and 2.2 million. Assumptions: i. mean compensation for those employed to carry out UN work (most of whom are in developing countries) is between $20,000 and $40,000; ii. the proportion of the budget spent on wages is between 75 per cent and 95 per cent; iii. the proportion of those whose salaries are covered by the UN budget who can be considered part of the UN's organizational culture is between 70 per cent and 95 per cent; iv. the peacekeeping budget may be discounted, as it pays for soldiers drawn from nation-state armies whose organizational identity may be very different.

36. World Bank (https://data.worldbank.org/indicator/IS.AIR.PSGR).
37. ISSP data can be reviewed and manipulated online at: http://zacat.gesis.org/.
38. In June 2018, Marine Le Pen's Front National renamed itself as Rassemblement National, in an echo of General Charles de Gaulle's Rassemblement du Peuple Français, which existed from 1947 until 1955.
39. 'Japan's Foreign Minister Champions International Tax System', *Nikkei Asian Review*, 27 August 2018 (accessed October 2018 at: https://asia.nikkei.com/Politics/Japan-s-foreign-minister-champions-international-tax-system).
40. Jane Perlez, 'With Blackface and Monkey Suit, Chinese Gala on Africa Causes Uproar', *The New York Times*, 16 February 2018.
41. Amartya Sen, *Identity and Violence: The Illusion of Destiny* (London: Allen Lane, 2006), p. 124.
42. Examples include Germany under the Nazis, Iraq throughout the twentieth century and Myanmar today.
43. See, for example, Branko Milanovic, *Global Inequality: A New Approach for the Age of Globalization* (Cambridge, Massachusetts: The Belknap Press of Harvard University Press, 2016).
44. 'A World of Free Movement Would be $78 Trillion Richer', *Economist*, 13 July 2017.
45. Steven Pinker, *Enlightenment Now: A Manifesto for Science, Reason, Humanism and Progress* (London: Penguin, 2018), p. 113.

PRINCIPLE 1: LEAVE NO ONE OUT

1. Giuseppe Mazzini, *Life and Writings of Joseph Mazzini* (London: Smith, Elder & Co., 1890), p. 169.

2. Kwame Anthony Appiah, *The Lies that Bind: Rethinking Identity*, (Profile Books, 2018), p. 73.

3. See for example Friedrich A. von Hayek, *The Road to Serfdom* (London: Routledge, 1944). His mention of 'civilized nations' on page 1 would surely today read 'the West'.

4. Bill Emmott, *The Fate of the West: The Battle to Save the World's Most Successful Political Idea* (New York: The Economist Books, 2017), p. 1.

5. See for example 'Ukraine is a Mess; the West Should Press It Harder to Fight Graft' (7 December 2017) and 'The West Should Help Saudi Arabia Limit Its War in Yemen' (15 October 2016). Under the current editor, this line has occasionally been modified by appeals for global action – a welcome change from the previous focus only on 'the West' as agents of change.

6. Australia is 'Western' despite being so far south that its name means 'land of the south' and its nickname is 'down under', while Morocco is definitely not 'Western', despite its official name, al-Maghrab, meaning 'land of the west'.

7. See, for example, G. John Ikenberry and Darren J. Liam, 'China's Emerging Institutional Statecraft: The Asian Infrastructure Investment Bank and the Prospects for Counter-hegemony', *Project on International Order and Strategy at Brookings*, April 2017.

8. *BBC News* story: 'Prom Dress Prompts "Cultural Appropriation" Row', 1 May 2018.

9. 'Chinese Dress at US Prom Wins Support in China after Internet Backlash', *South China Morning Post*, 1 May 2018.

10. See for example the predictions made in the popular book *When China Rules the World: The Rise of the Middle Kingdom and the End of the Western World* by Martin Jacques (London: Allen Lane, 2009).

11. I am referring to the most significant cultural shifts, comparable to those such as secularism, consumerism and individualism, which have shaped contemporary global culture. Of course, the more cosmetic elements of traditional European culture (e.g. pizza, Santa Claus) have also spread globally. We can expect cosmetic elements of other traditional cultures to continue to influence global culture, a process that is already well underway.

12. Anthony D. Smith, *Nations and Nationalism in a Global Era* (Cambridge: Polity, 1995), 19ff.

13. Yuval Noah Harari, *Sapiens: A Brief History of Humankind* (London: Harvill Secker, 2014), 24 ff.

14. See Ernest Gellner, *Nations and Nationalism* (Oxford: Blackwell, 1983), p. 56: 'nationalism is, essentially, the general imposition of a high culture on society ... it means that generalized diffusion of a school-mediated, academy-supervised idiom'.

15. This view was expressed to me by art historians whom I interviewed. Of course, the existence of different languages of expression in different artistic traditions should not be taken to imply that there was no borrowing or cross-pollination of ideas.

16. For Scotland, see: https://globaldimension.org.uk/resource/developing-global-citizens-within-curriculum-for-excellence/. For the others, see: http://www.unesco.org/new/en/member-states/single-view/news/four_countries_place_global_citizenship_education_as_curricu/.

17. Aviei Roshwald, 'The Post-1989 Era as Heyday of the Nation-State?', *International Journal of Politics Culture and Society,* 11 January 2011.

18. *BBC News* article: 'Donald Trump Retweets Far-right Group's Anti-Muslim Videos', 29 November 2017.

19. 'Can Simon Fuller's New Global Pop Band Emerge Triumphant in a Music Business "Going through Confusion"?', *Music Business Worldwide,* 18 September 2018.

20. However, in 2018 it was announced that Ridley Scott and Asif Kapadia are working on a documentary film version of Harari's *Sapiens* (https://www.hollywoodreporter.com/bookmark/ridley-scott-asif-kapadia-adapt-fiction-bestseller-sapiens-1126224).

21. Notwithstanding certain conventions that have been introduced to ensure a more inclusive film industry, for example that white actors should not play the parts of characters that depict people of colour.

PRINCIPLE 2: DEFINE THE MISSION, AND THE ENEMY

1. https://sustainabledevelopment.un.org/post2015/transformingourworld.

2. The full goals and targets can be found at http://www.undp.org/content/undp/en/home/sustainable-development-goals.html.

3. 'Awareness of Sustainable Development Goals (SDGs) vs Millennium Development Goals (MDGs)', Globescan report, August 2016 (accessed December 2018 at: https://globescan.com/wp-content/uploads/2017/07/Radar_eBrief_SDGvsMDG.pdf).

4. IPSOS Mori polling (https://www.ipsos.com/ipsos-mori/en-uk/maintaining-pride-nhs-challenge-new-nhs-chief-exec#note1).

5. The unusually strong commitment of many Japanese people to public cleanliness was highlighted when, after games in the 2018 World Cup, Japanese fans cleaned their part of the stadium, and the country's team cleaned their dressing room. Japanese people I spoke to agreed that this was a core part of national identity. CNN article: 'After Defeat, Japan's World Cup Team Leaves behind a Spotlessly Clean Locker Room and a "Thank You" Note', 3 July 2018 (accessed December 2018 at: https://edition.cnn.com/2018/07/03/football/japan-belgium-russia-thank-you-locker-room-trnd/index.html).

6. Specifically, the Global Goals that fall into this category are goal 1 (no poverty), goal 2 (no hunger), goal 3 (good health) goal 4 (quality education), goal 5 (gender equality), goal 6 (clean water and sanitation), goal 8 (good jobs and economic growth), goal 9 (innovation and infrastructure), goal 10 (reduced inequalities) and goal 17 (partnerships for the goals).

7. John Stauffer, Zoe Todd and Celeste-Marie Bernier, *Picturing Frederick Douglass: An Illustrated Biography of the Nineteenth Century's Most Photographed American* (New York: Liveright Publishing Corporation, 2015).

8. In 2017, total foreign aid measured by the OECD was $146.6 billion, of which $15.5 billion was humanitarian aid (http://www.oecd.org/development/development-aid-stable-in-2017-with-more-sent-to-poorest-countries.htm).

9. See for example Michael Clemens, 'Does Development Reduce Migration?', Centre for Global Development Working Papers (2014).

10. The foreign-aid programme of the United States is much more closely tied to self-interest, for example in giving contracts to US companies.

11. See for example the finding that 'the belief that all human beings belong to a single community' is strongly and positively correlated to support for foreign aid: http://chicagopolicyreview.org/2018/02/05/how-public-support-for-foreign-aid-depends-on-trust/.

12. Max Roser, 'The Short History of Global Living Conditions and Why It Matters that We Know It' (2018); published online at OurWorldIn-Data.org. Retrieved from: 'https://ourworldindata.org/a-history-of-global-living-conditions-in-5-charts'.

13. See for example http://blogs.worldbank.org/arabvoices/decline-child-mortality-rates-middle-east-north-africa-success-story.

14. In its first thirty years, Comic Relief raised over £1 billion in donations from the British public (https://www.bbc.co.uk/news/entertainment-arts-31874360).

15. https://globalgoalscast.org/creativity.
16. In 2000, foreign aid from China was around $1 billion (according to AidData, but disputed by some Chinese sources), and from Arab Gulf countries it was $600 million. South Korea gave $300 million, and Turkey gave an even smaller amount. Given total aid of $72 billion by the OECD donors (North America, Europe, Australia and Japan), this implies that China, Arab countries, Korea and Turkey together contributed less than 3 per cent of global aid in 2000. However, China's aid rose to average $10 billion in 2010–14 (according to AidData, but disputed by some Chinese sources). Arab Gulf countries averaged $6.3 billion in 2011–15, Korea averaged $1.6 billion in 2010–15 and Turkey averaged $5 billion in 2015–16. Given total aid of $131 billion from OECD donors in 2015, this implies China, Arab countries, Korea and Turkey together contributed as much as 15 per cent of global aid. Throughout this period, Brazil's foreign aid was relatively low. Sources: https://www.aiddata.org/china-official-finance; https://www.oecd.org/dac/dac-global-relations/Trends-in-Arab-concessional-financing-for-development.pdf; http://siteresources.worldbank.org/INTMENA/Resources/ADAPub82410web.pdf; https://data.oecd.org/oda/net-oda.htm; http://www.oecd.org/dac/stats/turkeys-official-development-assistanceoda.htm; https://www.devex.com/news/setting-its-own-course-brazil-foreign-aid-expands-and-evolves-78631; http://www.oecd.org/dac/korea.htm; and http://www.oecd.org/dac/financing-sustainable-development/development-finance-data/final-oda-2015.htm.
17. Karl Wolfgang Deutsch, *Nationalism and Its Alternatives* (New York: Knopf, 1969).
18. Just ten cities account for 10 per cent of the world's economy (https://financesonline.com/10-wealthiest-cities-in-the-world-its-not-new-york-or-london-at-the-top/). All of these cities could be reduced to rubble within the first hours of a major conflict.
19. Serhii Plokhy, *Chernobyl: History of a Tragedy* (London: Allen Lane, 2018).
20. Nafeez Ahmed, 'How the World Health Organisation Covered Up Iraq's Nuclear Nightmare', *Guardian*, 13 October 2013.
21. At the time of writing, the most prominent case was that of China's mass incarceration of Uyghur Muslims.
22. Josh Halliday, Lois Beckett and Caelainn Barr, 'Revealed: The Hidden Global Network behind Tommy Robinson', *Guardian*, 7 December 2018.

23. George Morgan, *Global Islamophobia: Muslims and Moral Panic in the West*, ed. Scott Poynting (Farnham: Ashgate, 2012), p. 1.
24. Both trace their origins to similar, though not identical, institutions in Ancient Greece. They can be called modern inventions in a meaningful sense, because of both the long period of discontinuity, and the significant differences, between the ancient and modern versions.
25. Pankaj Mishra, 'The Invention of the Hindu', *Axess* (2004).
26. Sarah Marsh, 'From Ali to Wyn: Names of Coming UK Winter Storms Revealed', *Guardian*, 12 September 2018.

PRINCIPLE 3: DEFEND THE NATION-STATE

1. The 1648 Peace of Westphalia, which closed the Thirty Years War in Central Europe, is often said to have established the principle of a world system based on sovereign states whose internal affairs could not be legitimately interfered with. While the true significance of the 1648 treaty in this regard has been questioned, the modern system of sovereign states is frequently referred to as the Westphalian system for this reason.
2. One writer who has been so bold as to argue for nation-states to be dissolved is Rana Dasgupta, who claimed in 2018 that 'the most momentous development of our era, precisely, is the waning of the nation-state', and that 'even if we wanted to restore what we once had, that moment is gone'. His proposed solution is a very different way of organizing the world, where there is unlimited mobility and 'the rights and opportunities accruing to western citizenship could be claimed far away', for example by Iraqis and Afghans being able to vote in US elections (after all, the outcome will affect them!). See 'The Demise of the Nation-State', *Guardian*, 6 April 2018.
3. Kohl's Speech at the Catholic University of Louvain, 1996.
4. Aviei Roshwald, 'The Post-1989 Era as the Heyday of the Nation-State', *International Journal of Politics, Culture and Society*, 11 January 2011.
5. OECD (https://data.oecd.org/gga/general-government-spending.htm).
6. 'Revenue Mobilization in Developing Countries', a 2011 paper by the International Monetary Fund, found at https://www.imf.org/external/np/pp/eng/2011/030811.pdf.
7. ISSP 2013.
8. Jonathan M. Powell and Clayton L. Thyne, 'Global Instances of Coups from 1950 to 2010: A New Dataset', *Journal of Peace Research*, 1 April 2011.

9. Max Roser and Mohamed Nagdy, 'Civil Wars' (2018); published online at OurWorldInData.org. Retrieved from: https://ourworldin data.org/civil-wars.

10. Eric Hobsbawm, *Nations and Nationalism since 1780: Programme, Myth, Reality* (Cambridge: Cambridge University Press, 1990), p. 145.

11. Ailsa Henderson, Charlie Jeffery and Daniel Wincott, *Citizenship after the Nation State: Regionalism, Nationalism and Public Attitudes in Europe* (Basingstoke: Palgrave Macmillan, 2014).

12. In 1954, the wording was changed to 'one Nation, under God'.

13. Our World In Data (https://ourworldindata.org/world-population-growth; accessed June 2018).

14. Sir John Strachey, *India, Its Administration and Progress* (3rd edn, 1903; 1st edn 1888; link to full text: https://archive.org/stream/in.ernet. dli.2015.278886/2015.278886.India-Its_djvu.txt; accessed June 2018).

15. Economist Intelligence Unit, 'Democracy Index 2017' (accessed in June 2018 at: http://www.eiu.com/Handlers/WhitepaperHandler. ashx?fi=Democracy_Index_2017.pdf&mode=wp&campaignid=De mocracyIndex2017).

PRINCIPLE 4: IF YOU LOVE MOBILITY, LET IT GO

1. Translation from C. R. Boxer, *The Christian Century in Japan*, 1549–1650 (Berkeley, LA: University of Chicago Press, 1951), pp. 439–40.

2. The continued view of Jewish people as not being a full part of the national community can be seen, for example, by the continuance of the Pale of Settlement (the limited area of the Russian empire where Jews were allowed to live), which was not abolished until the Bolshevik Revolution in 1917.

3. Ian Goldin, Geoffrey Cameron and Meera Balarajan, *Exceptional People: How Migration Shaped Our World and Will Define Our Future* (London: Blackwell, 2011), 58ff; and 'A History of Passports', *Wall Street Journal*, 17 October 2005 (https://www.wsj.com/articles/ SB112506690121624172).

4. Bryan Caplan and Vipul Naik, 'A Radical Case for Open Borders' (May 2014); link to full text: https://files.vipulnaik.com/openborders/ ARadicalCaseforOpenBorders.pdf; the paper also appeared in Benjamin Powell (ed.), *The Economics of Migration* (Oxford: OUP, 2015), Ch. 8, 180ff.

5. *Journal of Economic Perspectives*, vol. 25, no. 3, summer 2011, pp. 83–106.

6. David Goodhart, *The Road to Somewhere: Populist Revolt and the Future of Politics* (London: Penguin, 2017).

7. US 1970: census.gov/population/www/documentation/twps0029/tab13.html.
   US 2017: reuters.com/article/us-usa-immigration-data/u-s-foreign-born-population-swells-to-highest-in-over-a-century-idUSKCN1LT2HZ.
   UK 1971: Michael Rendall and John Salt (2005), 'The Foreign-born Population', Office for National Statistics.
   UK 2017: https://migrationobservatory.ox.ac.uk/resources/briefings/migrants-in-the-uk-an-overview/
   Germany 2017: https://www.theglobalist.com/where-immigrants-move-global-north-germany-united-states/.
   France and Germany historical: https://data.oecd.org/migration/foreign-born-population.htm.

8. https://news.gallup.com/poll/211883/number-potential-migrants-worldwide-tops-700-million.aspx.

9. Caplan and Naik, 'A Radical Case for Open Borders', op. cit.

10. Taxes paid by immigrants and remittances to their country of origin already do some work in redistributing their gains. Caplan and Naik (2014) are bullish about the feasibility of more radical measures to redistribute a larger part of the migrants' windfall in order to win political support from those otherwise opposed to free movement. Collier, in *Exodus: How Migration is Changing Our World* (London: Penguin, 2014) insists that it is politically unthinkable and morally undesirable to extract compensatory sums from migrants beyond their paying tax at the same rate as natives, as this would risk creating a permanent underclass in rich countries by making immigrants, often the poorest people, even poorer and encouraging the view that they should be treated differently.

11. Robert Putnam, '*E Pluribus Unum*: Diversity and Community in the Twenty-first Century (The 2006 Johan Skytte Prize Lecture)' in *Scandinavian Political Studies* (2006).

12. Sujin Jang, 'Cultural Brokerage and Creative Performance in Multicultural Teams', *Organization Science*, 28 December 2017.

13. Netflix, *House of Cards*, Chapter 15 (2014).

14. 'How the Slow Death of Labour Might Happen: A Dispatch from 2030', *Economist*, 2 February 2017.

15. Yascha Mounk and Roberto Stefan Foa, 'The Democratic Disconnect', *Journal of Democracy*, July 2016.

16. https://www.japantimes.co.jp/news/2018/11/02/national/major-policy-shift-japan-oks-bill-let-foreign-manual-workers-stay-permanently/#.XBTxIorqafA.
17. Source: Wikipedia, based on multiple sources. List of countries with numbers of foreign students in brackets: United States (1,043,839), China (489,200), United Kingdom (442,375), Canada (370,975), France (309,642), Australia (292,352) Russia (282,921), Germany (235,858), Japan (152,062), Spain (76,057).
18. https://www.theguardian.com/uk-news/2018/jan/04/tory-rebels-urge-may-remove-international-students-net-migration-figures.
19. http://blogs.worldbank.org/dev4peace/how-many-years-do-refugees-stay-exile.
20. Article 34 of the 1951 Convention Relating to the Status of Refugees, accessed July 2018 at: https://cms.emergency.unhcr.org/documents/11982/55726/Convention+relating+to+the+Status+of+Refugees+%28signed+28+July+1951%2C+entered+into+force+22+April+1954%29+189+UNTS+150+and+Protocol+relating+to+the+Status+of+Refugees+%28signed+31+January+1967%2C+entered+into+force+4+October+1967%29+606+UNTS+267/0bf3248a-cfa8-4a60-864d-65cdfece1d47.

PRINCIPLE 5: THE WINNERS MUST PAY TO PLAY

1. The OECD tax reform agenda is set out in Lee Corrick, 'Taxation of Multi-national Enterprises', in Thomas Pogge and Krishen Mehta (eds.), *Global Tax Fairness* (Oxford: Oxford University Press, 2016).
2. Thomas Piketty's proposal, which is for a higher, more redistributive levy than I am suggesting here, is set out in *Capital in the Twenty-first Century*, trans. Arthur Goldhammer (Harvard: Harvard University Press, 2014), Ch. 15.
3. CNBC article: 'Bill Gates has Paid over $10 billion in Taxes – Here's Why He Says He Should Pay More', 21 February 2018, accessed August 2018 at: https://www.cnbc.com/2018/02/21/bill-gates-has-paid-10-billion-in-taxes-and-says-he-should-pay-more.html.
4. See for example Michelle D'Arcy and Marina Nistotskaya 'The Early Modern Origins of Contemporary Tax Systems' (2015), accessed July 2018 at: https://ecpr.eu/Filestore/PaperProposal/fb909503-7fb8-4073-822a-a45dc3458e78.pdf.
5. Martin S. Daunton, *Trusting Leviathan* (London: Blackwell, 2001), Introduction.

6. K. K. Karaman, 'Another Divergence: Fiscal Centralization in Early Modern Europe', paper presented at the Eighth Conference of the European Historical Economics Society, 2009.

7. These institutions were not identical in each country: in England, the Parliament was a legislative body composed of elected commoners, aristocrats and bishops, while in France the Parlement de Paris, which approved new taxes, was a judicial appeal court populated only by nobles.

8. Tax rates were pretty much stable throughout the Ming and Qing dynasties, from the mid-fourteenth until the early-twentieth century. There was a consistent 3–4 per cent tax on income from land, and 2 per cent tax on commercial income, the latter of which rose only in the nineteenth century. Ray Huang (1998), 'The Ming Fiscal Administration', in Denis Twitchett and Frederick W. Mote (eds.), *The Ming Dynasty, 1398–1644, Part 2, The Cambridge History of China, Vol. 8* (Cambridge: Cambridge University Press, 1999); and H. Ramon Myers and Yeh-Chien Wang, (2002), 'Economic Developments, 1644–1800', in Willard Peterson, *The Ch'ing Empire to 1800, The Cambridge History of China, vol. 9* (Cambridge: Cambridge University Press, 2004).

9. It is a matter of some debate as to whether China independently of Europe became a 'nation' in the modern sense, but the consensus is that it did not. Sociologist Xiaotong Fei notes that: 'As a nation-in-itself, the Chinese nation emerged in confrontations between China and Western powers in the last century. But as a national-entity-of-consciousness, it has been shaped by thousands of years of historical process.' Xiaotong Fei, 'The Formation and Development of the Chinese Nation with Multi-ethnic Groups', *International Journal of Anthropology and Ethnology* (2017).

10. I refer here to Britain and not to England because during the period discussed Britain was under a single government. It is much debated whether and when English national identity was transferred to British national identity. This confusion speaks eloquently to the uncertainty and arbitrariness of the national myth.

11. Daunton, *Trusting Leviathan*, op. cit., Introduction.

12. Adam Smith, *An Inquiry into the Nature and Causes of the Wealth of Nations* (1776), Book 5, Ch. 2, 'Of Taxes', Appendix to Articles I & II.

13. Michael Kwass, *Privilege and Politics of Taxation in Eighteenth-century France* (London: Blackwell, 2001).

14. The foundational text of the Virginia School is James McGill Buchanan and Gordon Tullock, *The Calculus of Consent* (Ann Arbor: University of Michigan Press, 1962).

15. David F. Burg, *A World History of Tax Rebellions: An Encyclopedia of Tax Rebels, Revolts and Riots form Antiquity to the Present* (London/NY: Routledge, 2003), Introduction.

16. Smith, *An Inquiry*, op. cit., Book 5, Ch. 2.

17. Piketty, *Capital in the Twenty-first Century*, op. cit., Ch. 14.

18. Gabriel Zucman, *The Hidden Wealth of Nations* (Chicago: University of Chicago Press, 2015).

19. That is not to say that all is well for people living in tax havens. Zucman points out that most of the 50,000 citizens of Luxembourg have seen stagnating incomes for decades and have not benefitted materially from the wealth-management activities taking place in their tiny country.

20. CNBC article: 'The Last Time Companies Got a Break on Overseas Profits, It Didn't Work Out Well', 26 April 2017, accessed August 2018 at: https://www.cnbc.com/2017/04/26/what-happened-the-last-time-companies-got-a-break-on-overseas-profits.html.

21. World Bank, *Africa Pulse* (April 2017), p. 74, accessed August 2018 at: http://documents.worldbank.org/curated/en/348741492463112162/pdf/114375-REVISED-4-18-PMWB-AfricasPulse-Sping2017-vol15-ENGLISH-FINAL-web.pdf.

22. E. Crivelli, R. de Mooij and M. Keen. 'Base Erosion, Profit Shifting and Developing Countries', *FinanzArchiv: Public Finance Analysis*, 72(3), 268–301 (2016).

23. The figure normally quoted for total global aid is the sum of donations by members of the OECD DAC, which reached $146.6 billion in 2017 (see: http://www.oecd.org/newsroom/development-aid-stable-in-2017-with-more-sent-to-poorest-countries.htm). However, this does not include China or donors from the Middle East, whose aid is less public but conservatively adds another $10–20 billion to the total.

24. According to the World Bank, these reached $466 billion in 2017 (see: http://www.worldbank.org/en/news/press-release/2018/04/23/record-high-remittances-to-low-and-middle-income-countries-in-2017).

25. See especially Peter Dietsch and Thomas Rixen (eds.), *Global Tax Governance: What is Wrong with It and How to Fix It* (Colchester: ECPR Press, 2015), Ch. 2.

26. Dietsch and Rixen, op. cit., p. 33.

27. Joseph E. Stiglitz, *Globalization and Its Discontents Revisited: Anti-globalism in the Era of Trump* (New York: Norton, 2017), Introduction.

28. 'Budget 2010: Corporation Tax Slashed to 24p', *Guardian*, 22 June 2010 (retrieved August 2018 at: https://www.theguardian.com/uk/2010/jun/22/budget-2010-corporation-tax-slashed-to-24p).

29. *BBC News* article: 'Brexit: George Osborne Pledges to Cut Corporation Tax', 4 July 2016 (retrieved August 2018 at: https://www.bbc.co.uk/news/business-36699642).

30. 'Riddle of UK's Rising Corporation Tax Receipts', *Financial Times*, 26 April 2017 (retrieved August 2018 at: https://www.ft.com/content/ca3e5bd2-2a7e-11e7-9ec8-168383da43b7?desktop=true).

31. Germany until 1997 had a rate of 1 per cent on net wealth above 120,000DM ($71,000). See: https://www.boeckler.de/pdf/v_2017_11_10_bachleitner.pdf). Denmark until 1988 levied 2.2 per cent on wealth above the 98th percentile; the rate was halved in 1988 and abolished in 1997 (see: https://editorialexpress.com/cgi-bin/conference/download.cgi?db_name=NTA2017&paper_id=315).

32. https://harrisonbrook.co.uk/wealth-tax-spain-2018/.

33. Government of India, 'The Finance Act, 2015', in *Gazette of India* (accessed August 2018 at: http://www.egazette.nic.in/WriteRead Data/2015/163872.pdf).

34. https://uk.reuters.com/article/uk-france-tax/macron-fights-president-of-the-rich-tag-after-ending-wealth-tax-idUKKCN1C82DG.

35. Éric Pichet, a professor of economics and finance at Kedge Business School, claimed that the government was losing as much in revenue from the flight of wealthy people as it was bringing in from the tax, and furthermore that France's growth rate was 0.2 per cent lower as a result; https://www.ft.com/content/19feb16a-1aaf-11e7-a266-126724 83791a?desktop=true.

36. Piketty, *Capital in the Twenty-first Century*, op. cit.

37. John Lanchester, 'After the Fall', *London Review of Books*, 5 July 2018.

38. Branko Milanovic, *Global Inequality: A New Approach for the Age of Globalization* (Cambridge, Massachusetts: The Belknap Press of Harvard University Press, 2016), 103ff.

39. In Brazil, Pakistan and the Philippines, recent elections have focused on public anger against elites who are seen to have profited from international fraud involving tax havens.

40. Oxfam briefing report, 'Reward Work, Not Wealth', January 2018 (accessed August 2018 at: https://oxfamilibrary.openrepository.com/bitstream/handle/10546/620396/bp-reward-work-not-wealth-220118-en.pdf;jsessionid=9DEEB24D560CCBCECAD96C786F7CC27A?sequence=29).

41. Zucman, *Hidden Wealth of Nations*, op. cit.

42. Milanovic, *Global Inequality*, op. cit., p. 98.

43. Smith, *Wealth of Nations*, op. cit., Ch. 5, 'Of Taxes'.

44. Lee Corrick, 'Taxation of Multinational Enterprises', in Pogge and Mehta (eds.), op. cit.
45. For an explanation as to how this could work, see Zucman, *Hidden Wealth of Nations*, op. cit.
46. 'US Role in Global Economy Declines Nearly 50%', *Forbes*, 29 February 2016 (accessed August 2018 at: https://www.forbes.com/sites/mikepat ton/2016/02/29/u-s-role-in-global-economy-declines-nearly-50/).
47. Credit Suisse Research Institute, *The Credit Suisse Wealth Report 2017* (2018), accessed August 2018 at: https://www.credit-suisse. com/corporate/en/research/research-institute/publications.html.
48. Zucman, *Hidden Wealth of Nations*, op. cit., p. 49.
49. Samuel Moyn, *Not Enough: Human Rights in an Unequal World* (Cambridge, Massachusetts: The Belknap Press of Harvard University Press, 2018).
50. https://www.norway.no/en/missions/un/news/news-on-development-and-humanitarian-efforts/increase-in-norways-aid-budget-for-2018/.
51. Gabriel Zucman has claimed that such a register would be relatively straightforward to compile. Valuing shares in companies that are not publicly listed is far from easy, and real-estate values would have to be recalculated and regularly updated. But most financial wealth is already expressed in clear relation to its cash value.

PRINCIPLE 6: THE 'RULES-BASED SYSTEM' NEEDS BETTER RULES

1. Stephen C. Schlesinger, *Act of Creation: The Founding of the United Nations* (Boulder, CO/ Oxford: Westview, 2003), p. 6.
2. Wendell L. Willkie, *One World* (Cassell and Company, 1943), see p. 1.
3. Schlesinger, *Act of Creation*, op. cit., p. 8.
4. David M. Malone, *The UN Security Council: From the Cold War to the 21st Century* (Boulder, CO/London, Lynne Rienner, 2004), p. 6.
5. See for example Madeleine O. Hosli et al. 'Squaring the Circle? Collective and Distributive Effects of United Nations Security Council Reform', 29 March 2011.
6. Tom Miles, 'World Trade's Top Court Close to Breakdown as U.S. Blocks Another Judge', *Reuters*, 26 September 2018.
7. After it was not granted a seat on the Security Council in 2005, Japan significantly reduced its UN financial contributions. In 2018, Shinzō Abe ended his speech at the UN General Assembly by stating that 'in

light of the lack of progress in reforming the Security Council, the significance of the United Nations in the twenty-first century world is already being starkly questioned'; see 'Full text of Prime Minister Abe's speech at UN' in *Mainichi*, 26 September 2018.

8. Schlesinger, *Act of Creation*, op. cit., p. 290.

9. Mark Malloch-Brown, *The Unfinished Global Revolution* (London: Allen Lane, 2011).

10. Interview with author.

11. Anne-Marie Slaughter, *A New World Order* (Sage, 2005), p. 8.

12. *Ibid.*, p. 29.

13. Kwame Anthony Appiah, *Cosmopolitanism: Ethics in a World of Strangers* (London: Allen Lane, 2006), p. 163.

14. Slaughter, *A New World Order*, op. cit., p. 8.

15. Max Weber, 'Politics as a Vocation', *Lectures to the Munich Free Students Union* (1919).

16. *Oxford English Dictionary.*

17. See for example the speech by George Sabra, leader of the Syrian National Coalition, in April 2013, where he said, 'The United Nations and human rights organizations must act immediately to address these atrocities. The Syrian people are human beings too and Syria is a member of several international organizations . . . We intend to submit this issue to the General Assembly to get a resolution. We also asked the Friends of Syria to try and obtain a Security Council Resolution to stop the death of Syrians by Scud missiles' (accessed September 2013 at: http://en.etilaf.org/press/remarks-by-mr-george-sabra.html).

18. See note 6.

19. 'Qianlong Letter to George III (1792)'. University of California, Santa Barbara, accessed September 2018 at: http://www.history.ucsb.edu/faculty/marcuse/classes/2c/texts/1792QianlongLetterGeorgeIII.htm.

20. G. John Ikenberry, *After Victory: Institutions, Strategic Restraint, and the Rebuilding of Order after Major Wars* (London: Blackwell, 2001), 167ff.

21. G. John Ikenberry, 'Global Security Cooperation in the Twenty-first Century', in Joseph E. Stiglitz and Mary Kaldor (eds.), *The Quest for Security: Protection without Protectionism and the Challenge of Global Governance* (NY: Colombia University Press, 2013).

22. John Stuart Mill, *Considerations on Representative Government* (1864).

23. *Ibid.*

24. Mekuria Bulcha, 'The Politics of Linguistic Homogenization in Ethiopia and the Conflict over the Status of "Afaan Oromo"', *African Affairs*, 1 July 1997.

25. See for example Tom Gardner and Charlie Rosser, '"Abiy Ahmed is Our Miracle": Ethiopia's Democratic Awakening', *Guardian*, 25 September 2018 (accessed September 2018 at: https://www.theguardian.com/global-development/2018/sep/25/abiy-ahmed-miracle-ethiopia-democratic-awakening).

26. Where resettling refugees presents cultural obstacles, countries could fulfil their obligations financially by providing sufficient compensation to states which are prepared to resettle them. Properly compensating receiving countries would require a greater contribution per refugee than the current modest amounts given to UNHCR.

27. https://globescan.com/global-citizenship-a-growing-sentiment-among-citizens-of-emerging-economies-global-poll/.

28. See for example Malloch-Brown, *The Unfinished Global Revolution*, op. cit., 191ff; Hosli et al., 'Squaring the Circle?', op. cit.; Frances Stewart and Sam Daws, 'An Economic and Social Security Council at the UN', *QEH Working Paper 68* (March 2001); and José Antonio Ocampo, 'Rethinking Global Economic and Social Governance', in Stiglitz and Kaldor (eds.), *The Quest for Security*, op. cit., 332ff.

29. Certainty does not guarantee justice but it allows the participants in the system to navigate their interests more effectively than if there were no clear rules. Certainty greatly reduces the risk of conflict, even in an unjust system. My friends and family who lived through Iraq's most challenging years tell me that this was the main advantage of Saddam Hussein's brutal rule in comparison with what followed. Before 2003, most people knew whom to fear, whom to avoid, what not to say – in short, how to stay alive. After the war, the coming and going of a dizzying array of gangs, militias, hit squads and vigilantes, each with shifting allegiances, meant that figuring out how to survive on a daily basis got much harder. Of course, there was a great deal of uncertainty under the arbitrary power of the old regime, but far more after it was removed.

30. By the late eighteenth century, the flexible parliamentary model had become so powerful that Britain, despite having a mad king who was eventually confined to a lunatic asylum, experienced a period of unprecedented growth, stability and global influence. The last time a king had lost his mind, in the 1400s, a bloody civil war – the Wars of the Roses – had resulted. Until the nineteenth century, only a small

minority of people had the vote, so parliament was not really about justice and democracy in the modern sense – there was little protection for the poorer masses at home, let alone colonial subjects. But a clear system emerged for allowing changes in the power of individuals and groups to be reflected in politics, and for the substitution of leaders who did not have the confidence of the most important constituencies for those who did.

31. As David Held comments: 'the architects of the post-war order did not, in most cases, design institutions that would organically adjust to fluctuations in national power', *Elements of a Theory of Global Governance* (Sage, 2017).

32. See note 6.

33. Ian Goldin, *Divided Nations: Why Global Governance is Failing and What We Can Do about It* (Oxford: Oxford University Press, 2013).

34. The EU term is 'qualified majority', defined as a decision that meets both of the following criteria: a) counting each country as a single vote, agreement by 55 per cent of countries, or 72 per cent of countries if the proposal is neither from the European Commission or the High Representative for Foreign Affairs and Security Policy, b) agreement by countries representing 65 per cent of the EU's population.

35. At the time of writing, this was a matter of hot debate. The new president, Jimmy Morales, seemed determined to shut down the body, but was finding this difficult because it was so popular with the Guatemalan people. See 'Guatemala's Government Races to Scrap an Anti-corruption Commission', *Economist,* 13 September 2018.

36. United Nations, *World Summit Outcome Document* (2005).

37. This would, however, require the treaties themselves to be redrafted and re-ratified.

CONCLUSION: A CHOICE OF PATHS

1. Wang Hui, *China from Empire to Nation-State,* trans. Michael Gibbs Hill (Harvard: Harvard University Press, 2014), p. 27.

2. Rian Thum, 'China's Mass Internment Camps Have No Clear End in Sight', *Foreign Policy,* 22 August 2018.

3. For the *Nineteen Eighty-Four* comparison, see Rachel Botsman, 'Big Data Meets Big Brother as China Moves to Rate Its Citizens', *Wired. com,* 21 October 2018 (accessed October 2018 at: https://www.wired. co.uk/article/chinese-government-social-credit-score-privacy-invasion);

for the *Black Mirror* comparison see Alice Vincent, 'Black Mirror is Coming True in China, Where Your "Rating" Affects Your Home, Transport and Social Circle', *Telegraph*, 15 December 2017.

4. See for example 'Across China: Credit System Provides Support for Social Development', *XinhuaNet*, 3 July 2018 (accessed October 2018 at: http://www.xinhuanet.com/english/2018-07/03/c_137298542.htm).

5. For example, from 1127 until 1279, the Han Chinese heartland was split between the Jin and Southern Song dynasties.

6. According to the 2010 census, the Han population in China was 1.2 billion, or 91.5 per cent. See 'Communiqué of the National Bureau of Statistics of People's Republic of China on Major Figures of the 2010 Population Census', National Bureau of Statistics, 28 April 2011 (accessed October 2018 at: https://web.archive.org/web/20131108022004/http://www.stats.gov.cn/english/newsandcomingevents/t20110428_402722244.htm).

7. 'Is India an Outlier When It Comes to Tax–GDP Ratio?', *LiveMint*, 23 January 2018 (https://www.livemint.com/Industry/7UAyR2aM3Yh8rBe TD28WHL/Is-India-an-outlier-when-it-comes-to-taxGDP-ratio.html).

Index

Abe, Shinzō 137, 172–3n7
Abiy Ahmed 133–4
Abyssinia see Ethiopia
academia:
  foreign students 20, 24, 96,
    168n17
  globalization of 20, 96
AfD (Alternative für Deutschland)
  6, 23, 83
Afghanistan 29, 148
Africa:
  agriculture, early development
    of 35
  Arab nationalism 10, 41, 144–5
  economic growth 20
  foreign aid to 53–4, 58
  industrialization 15
  taxation and tax avoidance
    107, 108
  see also Angola; Central
    African Republic;
    Democratic Republic of
    Congo; Egypt; Ghana;
    Morocco; South Africa;
    Tunisia
agriculture, early development 35
Ahmed, Riz 45
air travel 21
Al-Qaeda 6
Alternative für Deutschland (AfD)
  6, 23, 83
Amaziq (ethnic group) 145

Amazon (technology company),
    tax arrangements 112, 114
American Sniper (film) 45, 46
Andhra Pradesh 77
Angola 72
'animist' religions 65
anti-slavery movement 50, 51
Appiah, Kwame Anthony 31, 37,
    85, 126, 133
Arab League 146
Arab nationalism 10, 16, 31–2, 41,
    59, 95, 144–6
Argentina 28
art 37, 43–4, 162n15
Asante people 37
Australia 32, 87, 91, 98, 161n6,
    168n17

Bangladesh 54, 149
Base Erosion and Profit Shifting
    (BEPS) 114
Berlin, wartime bombing 64
Berlin Wall, fall of 68
Bermuda 110
Bharatiya Janata Party
    (India) 76
Black Mirror (television series)
    148
Bolivarianism 10
Bolshevik Revolution (1917) 106,
    166n2
Bolton, John 124

Brazil:
  education 16
  elections 28–9, 113, 171*n*39
  foreign aid 55, 164*n*16
Brexit (British exit from European
    Union) 4, 71, 80, 83, 84, 90,
    93–4, 109, 139, 158*n*20
Britain:
  anti-immigration views 83, 84,
    90, 93–4
  Brexit 4, 71, 80, 83, 84, 90,
    93–4, 109, 139, 158*n*20
  economic and political
    injustice, views on 28–9
  education 16, 168*n*17
  foreign aid 120
  global citizenship, views on 22
  immigrant population 84, 90
  Iraq invasion (2003) 13, 129,
    131
  monarchy 40, 103, 137
  National Health Service (NHS)
    49, 50, 53
  national identity 39, 53, 132–3,
    169*n*10
  parliamentary system 104, 137,
    169*n*7, 174–5*n*30
  social media usage 159*n*28
  state, growth of 69
  taxation 103, 104, 106, 109–10,
    112, 114
  transport 19–20
  UN Security Council
    membership 137
  voting systems 139
  see also England; Scotland
British Virgin Islands 106
Brittany 39, 74
Buddhism 14
Buffett, Warren 102

Bulcha, Mekuria 133
Bush, George W. 107, 109, 130

Canada 168*n*17
Cantonese people 94, 147
Caplan, Bryan, 'A Radical Case
    for Open Borders' 82–3, 87,
    92, 99, 167*n*10
Caracalla, Roman Emperor 14
Catalonia 74
Cayman Islands 107
Central African Republic 29
'certainty', as political attribute
    136–7, 174*n*29
Chan Zuckerberg Initiative 4
Chernobyl nuclear accident
    (1986) 60
China:
  agriculture, early development
    of 35
  and cultural 'appropriation' 36, 37
  economic rise 6, 27, 34, 38, 54,
    61, 147
  education and academia 16, 18,
    20, 24, 168*n*17
  ethnic groups 6, 147, 164*n*21,
    176*n*5–6
  foreign aid 55, 56, 164*n*16,
    170*n*23
  foreigners, views on 24
  global citizenship, views on 24
  and global government 127
  hukou system 99
  Imperial era 103, 130, 146, 147,
    169*n*8, 176*n*5
  internal migration 99, 147
  and international financial
    institutions 56, 71
  languages 17, 18, 94, 147
  military threat 61, 62, 63

nationalist movements 59, 146–7
nationhood, development of 103, 146–9, 169n9
poverty reduction 54, 147
racial stereotyping 25
refugees, views on 135–6
religion 65
Social Credit System 148
social media usage 19
state control 70, 73, 147–8
taxation 103, 118, 169n8
television 25
transport 20
and 'Western' model 27, 34, 35
Xi government 113
Christianity 14, 15, 34, 89
civil wars, casualty totals 73
Civilisations (television series) 43
Clegg, Sir Nick 4
Clemens, Michael 83, 163n9
climate change 2, 7, 64, 65, 78, 128–9, 135, 144, 146
Cold War 68, 123
Collier, Paul, Exodus 87–8, 167n10
Colombia 44, 72
Comic Relief (fundraising initiative) 54, 163n14
Communism 4, 74, 106, 123
conflict, international:
    global goals on ending 48
    and nationalism 58–60
    public views on 25–6
    threats of 58–62, 64–5
Congo, Democratic Republic of 52, 72
Constantine the Great, Roman Emperor 34
corporation tax 108–10, 111–12, 114–15

coups d'etat, numbers of 73
Crimea, Russian annexation 129
cryptocurrencies 23–4
Cuba, emigration to Florida 91
cultural appropriation, notions of 36–7
Curtis, Richard 54–5
cyber warfare 62, 135

Dasgupta, Rana 165n2
democratic politics:
    and avoidance of violence 63–4
    development of 2, 27, 165n24
    and notions of 'the West' 33, 35
    public support for 94
    threats to 78–80
    see also referenda
Democratic Republic of Congo 52, 72
Denmark, taxation 110, 171n31
Deutsch, Karl Wolfgang, Nationalism and its Alternatives 59
DiEM25 (Democracy in Europe Movement 2025) 4
Diogenes the Cynic 46
disease prevention see health care and disease prevention
Douglass, Frederick 50
dual citizenship 30–31
Duterte, Rodrigo 23

Ebola (virus disease) 2
'echo chambers' (social media) 19, 158–9n27–8
Economist, The (newspaper) 32, 83, 161n5
    Intelligence Unit's Democracy Index 79

education:
  and globalism 11–12, 22, 24,
    44, 146
  international league tables 16
  and nationalism 15–16, 43
  see also academia; literacy;
    teaching
Egypt 6, 79, 145–6, 157*n*15
Emmott, Bill, *The Fate of the West*
  32
England 11, 132
  national identity 39, 42, 169*n*10
  parliamentary system 103, 137,
    169*n*7
  taxation 103
  see also Britain
English:
  as global lingua franca 17–18,
    146, 158*n*20
  and notions of 'the West' 33
environmental protection:
  global-enforcement powers 5,
    25, 128–9, 135
  UN Global Goals 48, 59, 64
  see also climate change
Erdoğan, Recep Tayyip 6
Ethiopia 54, 72, 73, 133–4
ethnic cleansing 41, 62–3, 75, 149
European Union (EU) 68, 71, 93,
    145
  British exit 4, 71, 80, 83, 84,
    90, 93–4, 109, 139, 158*n*20
  defence spending and military
    interventions 61
  development of union 75–6,
    79–80
  Lisbon Treaty ratification
    79–80
  'qualified majorities' 139,
    175*n*34

and tax reform 107, 114, 135
use of English 158*n*20
extraterrestrials, perceived threats
  of 65

Facebook (social media company)
  18, 44
FATCA (United States Foreign
  Account Tax Compliance
  Act) 115–16
Fei Xiaotong 169*n*9
Fidesz party (Hungary) 6, 42, 83
film industry 45–6, 65, 161*n*21
financial crisis (2008) 19,
    101, 112
fine art 37, 43–4, 162*n*15
Finland 83, 110
First World War 124
'flexibility', as political attribute
    137–8
Florida 91
Foa, Roberto Stefan, 'The
  Democratic Disconnect' 94
Fonsi, Luis, 'Despacito' 158*n*25
food supplies 48, 52, 53–4, 97
foreign aid 51–7, 163*n*8–11,
    164*n*16, 170*n*23
  emerging-market donors 55–6
  public views on 3, 51, 119,
    155*n*6, 163*n*11
  and taxation 3, 28, 51, 53, 57,
    119–20, 138, 155*n*6
France:
  anti-immigration views 83, 84
  European Constitution
    referendum (2005) 79
  foreign students 168*n*17
  immigrant population 84
  Napoleonic Wars 10, 59
  national identity 39, 42

parliamentary system 103, 169*n*7

Rassemblement National 23, 83, 160*n*38

regional identity 74

Revolution 9, 10, 104–5, 111, 121, 156*n*2

Revolutionary Wars 10, 11

state, growth of 69

taxation 103, 104–5, 106, 111, 171*n*35

UN Security Council membership 137

see also Nice

free movement 49, 68, 81–99, 167*n*10

Fuller, Simon 45

Fusco, Idamaria, 'The Unification of Italy' 158*n*23

G20 134

and tax reform 114, 116

Garibaldi, Giuseppe 157*n*17

Gates, Bill 102

Gaulle, Charles de 160*n*38

Gellner, Ernest, *Nations and Nationalism* 155*n*3, 162*n*14

gender equality 24, 48, 57–8

gentrification 99

George III, King 130, 137, 174*n*30

Georgia 29

Germany:

AfD (Alternative für Deutschland) 6, 23, 83

foreign students 168*n*17

global citizenship, views on 22

global governance, views on 128, 130

and Greek debt crisis 3, 156*n*8

immigrant population 84

language 17, 40–41

national identity 40–41

Nazism 31, 41, 130, 160*n*42

regional identity 74

reunification 3

taxation 110, 171*n*31

UN Global Goals, public awareness of 48

unification 5, 16, 40–41, 59, 95

see also Berlin; Prussia

Ghana 37

Gibran, Gibran Khalil vii

global citizenship:

public views on 4–5, 22–6

teaching of 11–12, 44

global enforcement powers 123, 135–41

public views on 5, 25–6, 128–9

Global Goals, UN Declaration of (2015) 7, 47, 48–59, 64, 119, 140–41, 144, 163*n*6

public awareness of 48, 54–5

global government, ideas and possibilities of 7, 12, 46, 122–42, 148

Globespan World Values Survey 22–3

Goethe, Johann Wolfgang von 11

Goldin, Ian 138

Goodhart, David, *The Road to Somewhere* 84

Google (technology company), tax arrangements 110

Greece, ancient 61, 165*n*24

gods 65

Greece, modern, debt crisis 3, 28, 156*n*8

Guam 138

Guatemala 141
    International Commission
        against Impunity 141,
        175*n*35

Haiti 87
Hammond, Philip 109
Harari, Yuval Noah:
    Homo Deus 43
    Sapiens 42, 43, 162*n*20
health care and disease prevention
    2, 7, 29, 49, 50, 51, 54, 57,
    65, 70, 135, 144
Held, David 175*n*31
Herder, Johann Gottfried 40–41
Hinduism 65
Hiroshima, atomic bombing 64
history (academic discipline),
    'world history' 43
*History of the World in 100
    Objects* (podcast) 43
Hizbollah (Islamist militant group)
    72
Homeland (television series) 45
Hong Kong 147
Houellebecq, Michel, *Submission*
    84
House of Cards (television series)
    93
Huguenots 39
hukou system (China) 99
Hungary, Fidesz party 6, 42, 83

Iceland 110
Ignotus, Paul 1
Ikenbery, John 130–31
immigration 51–2, 70, 82–99,
    167*n*10
India:
    anti-immigration views 85
    audiovisual media 24
    economic rise 27, 38, 61, 137,
        149
    ethnic cleansing 41, 75, 149
    ethnic, religious and tribal
        groups 75, 76–8, 149, 150
    global citizenship, views on 4,
        22, 23, 24
    global governance, views on
        128
    independence and partition 75,
        76, 77, 137, 149
    international conflict, views on
        25
    languages 17, 76, 77
    Maoist insurgencies 72, 150
    Modi government 23, 42, 76
    Mogul Empire 130
    national identity and
        development of nationhood
        17, 75, 76–8, 95, 149–51
    newspapers 18
    sanitation services 150
    state, growth of 70
    state boundaries,
        reorganization of 77–8
    taxation 111, 150
    transport 20
    UN Global Goals, public
        awareness of 48
    and 'Western' model 27, 34
Indonesia 48, 54, 70
Industrial Revolution 2, 15
inter-governmental networks 134–5
International Committee of the
    Red Cross 30
International Court of Justice 141
    US withdrawal 130
International Criminal Court 130
International Monetary Fund 71

international non-governmental
    organizations (INGOs),
    growth of 20–21
International Social Survey
    Programme (ISSP) 22, 25–6,
    70, 71–2, 77, 128
Iran 32
    nuclear deal 61
Iraq 35, 52, 146, 157n15, 160n42,
    174n29
    ethnic and religious groups 30,
    31–2
    invasion and civil war 13,
    29, 32, 60, 69, 72,
    129, 131, 134, 148,
    174n29
Ireland:
    Lisbon Treaty ratification 79
    taxation 110
Islam and Islamism 6, 14, 72, 84,
    145
    see also Muslims
Islamic State 6, 62
Islamophobia 62–3
Israel 41, 59, 84, 129
ISSP see International Social
    Survey Programme
Istanbul 34
Italy:
    La Lega 80, 83
    language 17, 41
    newspapers 18, 158n23
    unification 11, 41, 59, 95, 132,
    158n23

Japan:
    cleanliness, pride in 49, 53,
    163n5
    defence spending 61
    foreign students 168n17

foreigners, views on 95
global citizenship, views on 22
global governance, views on
    128, 130
global policies 23
immigrant population 95
language 17
national identity 49, 53, 163n5
nationalist movements 59
Second World War 64, 130
state, growth of 69
transport 20
and United Nations 124,
    172–3n7
and 'Western' model 32
Jews 31, 84, 166n2
Jordan 146
Julius Caesar 46
Justinian I, Byzantine Emperor 37

Kant, Immanuel 12, 40, 46
Kapadia, Asif 162n20
Kohl, Helmut 68
Korea see South Korea
Kurds 31, 145

Lanchester, John, 'After the Fall'
    112
language:
    and nationalism 10, 15, 16–18,
    30, 40–41, 94, 132, 133, 145
    teaching 16, 17–18, 146
Le Pen, Marine 160n38
League of Nations 20, 124
Lebanon 35, 72
Lega, La (Italy) 80, 83
Lennon, John, 'Imagine' 122
Libya 29, 138
Lisbon Treaty (European Union)
    79–80

literacy 15, 16, 18, 43
local communities 13, 63, 74, 85–6
  and gentrification 99
  and immigrant populations
    88–9, 99
Luxembourg 106, 107, 110, 112,
    135, 170n19

MacGregor, Neil, *A History of the
    World in 100 Objects* 43
Macron, Emmanuel 111
Malloch-Brown, Mark, Baron
    124–5, 128, 138
Mandarin (language) 17, 94
Manila, wartime bombing 64
Maoism 72, 150
Marxism 14, 74
mass media:
  and globalism 43, 44–5
  and nationalism 18–19
mathematics teaching 16
May, Theresa 12, 109
Mazzini, Giuseppe 11, 30, 47
Menelik II, Emperor of Ethiopia
    133
MeToo movement (anti-sexual
    abuse campaign) 19
Mexico 128
  secession of Texas 91, 92
Milanovic, Branko, *Global
    Inequality* 113
Mill, John Stuart 132
Miller, David 85
Mishra, Pankaj, 'The Invention of
    the Hindu' 65
mobility:
  free movement 49, 68, 81–99,
    167n10
  transportation developments
    19–20, 21

see also immigration; refugees
Modi, Narendra 23, 42
Mogul Empire 130
monarchies 9–10, 40, 102–3, 104,
    105, 136, 137
Mongolia 44, 65
Morales, Jimmy 175n35
Morgan, George, *Global
    Islamophobia* 63
Morocco 144, 145, 161n6
Mounk, Yascha, 'The Democratic
    Disconnect' 94
Moyn, Samuel, *Not Enough* 118
Mozambique 72
Murray, Douglas, *The Strange
    Death of Europe* 84
music 36, 45
Muslim Brotherhood 6, 79
Muslims:
  anti-Muslim movements 62–3
  in China 147, 164n21
  and immigration 84
  in India 75, 76–7, 149
  rejection of globalism 6, 27, 34
  terrorism 6, 27, 61, 62
  see also Islam and Islamism
Myanmar 29, 31, 41, 160n42

NAFTA (North American Free
    Trade Agreement) 71
Nagasaki, atomic bombing 64
Naik, Vipul, 'A Radical Case for
    Open Borders' 82–3, 87, 92,
    99, 167n10
Naples 132
Napoleon III, Emperor 158n17
Napoleonic Wars 10, 59
Nasser, Gamal Abdel 145
National Health Service (Britain;
    NHS) 49, 50, 53

nationalization:
  of industry 70
  of property 106
Native Americans 75, 76, 91
Nazism 31, 41, 130, 160*n*42
Nepal 72
Netherlands 79
networks, inter-governmental
  134–5
New Zealand 113
newspapers, and nationalism 18,
  158*n*23
NHS *see* National Health
  Service
Nicaragua, US covert operations
  130
Nice (France) 157–8*n*17
Nigeria 16, 24, 27, 34
Norway 118
  foreign aid 120
Now United (pop group) 45
nuclear energy 47
nuclear fusion/fission, comparisons
  with 47
nuclear weapons and warfare 60,
  61–2, 64, 129, 164*n*18

Obama Foundation 4
OECD (Organization for
  Economic Co-operation and
  Development) 164*n*16
  PISA initiative 16
  and taxation reform 114, 116
Ohmae, Keniche, *The End of the
  Nation State* 67–8
Olympic Games, London (2012)
  49
open borders *see* free movement
Opium Wars 130
Orbán, Viktor 6, 42

Organization for Economic Co-
  operation and Development
  see OECD
Oromo people 133–4
Orwell, George, *Nineteen Eighty-
  Four* 148
Osborne, George 109
Osei Bonsu, King of the Asante 37
Ostler, Nicholas 18
Ottoman Empire 15, 145, 157*n*12
Oxfam, 'Reward Work, Not
  Wealth' briefing report 113

Pakistan 28–9, 41, 63, 85, 149,
  150
  elections 113, 171*n*39
Palaeolithic groups 42
Panama 107
Panama Papers scandal
  (2015) 113
patriotism 12–13
personification of danger 65–6
Peter the Great, Tsar 15
pharmaceuticals 35, 93
Philippines 51
  economic growth 73
  elections 28–9, 113, 171*n*39
  views on global and national
    identity 4, 22, 23, 25, 73
  see also Manila
Phoenicians 35
Pichet, Éric 171*n*35
Piketty, Thomas 101, 112, 168*n*2
Pinker, Steven, *Enlightenment
  Now* 27–8
PISA (Programme for
  International Student
  Assessment) 16
Plato, *Statesman* 143
pop music 36, 45

power generation 47
  privatization 70
Presley, Elvis 36
privatization, of industry 70, 71
Project Everyone (campaigning
  organization) 54–5
Prussia 11, 16, 40
Putin, Vladimir 113
Putnam, Robert 13, 88–90, 94

Qianlong, Emperor 130

racism 6, 11, 12, 25, 38, 85, 89
railways 19–20, 21
  privatization 70
Rassemblement National (France)
  23, 83, 160n38
Red Cross, International
  Committee of the 30
refugees 73, 78, 82, 86, 96–9,
  135–6, 174n26
regional identity 74, 132
religion:
  and globalism 14
  and nationalism 10
  and personification of danger
    65
  see also Buddhism;
    Christianity; Hinduism;
    Islam
renationalization, of industry 71
'respect for difference', as political
  attribute 140–41
Riall, Lucy, Garibaldi 158n23
Riesbeck, Johann Kaspar 5
Rohingya people 31
romantic nationalism 31, 40–42,
  43, 47
Rome, ancient 14
  gods 65

Roosevelt, Franklin D. 122, 123
Roshwald, Aviei 68
Russia, post-Soviet:
  annexation of Crimea 129
  economic rise 61
  foreign election interference 19
  foreign students 168n17
  intervention in Syria 62
  and notions of 'the West' 32
  state control 73
  and United Nations 48, 124
Russia, pre-Soviet 15, 157n13
  abolition of serfdom 81
  Bolshevik Revolution 106,
    166n2
  Jewish population 166n2
Russian Orthodox Church 15
Rwanda 29

Sabra, George 173n17
San Francisco conference (1945)
  123, 124
science fiction 65, 148
Scotland:
  global citizenship, views on
    11–12, 44
  nationalists and independence
    movement 11–12, 44, 74,
    132–3
Scott, Sir Ridley 162n20
Second World War 60–61, 64, 68,
  73, 122–3, 130
'selective inclusiveness', as political
  attribute 138–9
Sen, Amartya, Identity and
  Violence 26–7, 155n2
Serbia 29, 34
serfdom, abolition of 10, 81
Shinawatra, Thaksin 78
Sicily 132

silk production 37
Slaughter, Anne-Marie 126, 133, 134
slavery 91
  anti-slavery movement 50, 51
  see also serfdom
Smith, Adam 104, 105–6, 113
Smith, Anthony D., *Nations and Nationalism in a Global Era* 38–9
Social Credit System (China) 148
social media 18–19, 44–5
  'echo chambers' 19, 158–9*n*27–8
South Africa 25, 128
South Korea 55, 164*n*16
space exploration 65
Spain 74, 110, 168*n*17
Spice Girls (pop group) 45
sport 63, 64, 165*n*24
  FIFA World Cup 19, 163*n*5
  Olympic Games 49
Sreeramulu, Potti 77
steel production 70
Stockton–Darlington railway 19–20
storms, naming of 66
Strachey, Sir John, *India, Its Administration and Progress* 76
Strange, Susan, *The Retreat of the State* 67–8
Sun Yat-Sen 147
Sunstein, Cass 158*n*27
supermajority (voting system) 139–40, 175*n*34
Sweden, taxation 103, 110
Switzerland 10, 106, 132
Syria 145
  civil war 29, 51, 62, 72, 73, 173*n*17
  emigration and refugees 52, 136

taxation 28, 78, 100–121, 135, 167*n*10
  corporation tax 108–10, 111–12, 114–15
  and foreign aid 3, 28, 51, 53, 57, 119–20, 138, 155*n*6
  tax havens/avoidance 106–8, 110, 112, 113, 114, 117, 121, 135, 170*n*19, 171*n*39
  wealth tax 57, 101–2, 110–11, 117–21, 138, 171*n*31, 172*n*51
teaching:
  foreign languages 16, 17–18, 146
  global citizenship 11–12, 44
  global goals and values 55, 65–6
  mathematics 16
television 24, 25, 43, 45–6
Tennyson, Alfred, 1st Baron, 'Locksley Hall' 122, 123, 142
terrorism 61
  and foreign aid 51–2
  and immigration 91–2
  war on terror 62–3
Texas 44, 91, 92
Thailand 78–9
Thirty Years War 165*n*1
'Thucydides trap' 61
Thuringia 74
Tibet 146, 147
TIMSS (Trends in International Mathematics and Science Study) 16
Tocqueville, Alexis de, *The Old Regime and the Revolution* 100

Tokugawa Iemitsu, Shogun 81
Truman, Harry S. 122, 123, 124
Trump, Donald 4, 23, 131
  'America First' 42
  border controls 83
  and international organizations
    123–4, 129
  racism 6
  social media use 44
  supporters 6, 83
  tax policies 107, 109
  trade wars 83
Tunisia 98
Turkey 6, 25, 34, 41, 70, 145
  foreign aid 55, 164n16
  see also Ottoman Empire

Uganda 44
UK see Britain
UKIP (UK Independence Party)
  94
Ukraine 29, 30, 69, 129
UN (United Nations) 122–5
  Charter 124, 137, 141
  formation 60, 64, 122–3
  Global Goals declaration (2015)
    7, 47, 48–59, 64, 119,
    140–41, 144, 163n6
  reform 7, 124–5, 138,
    142, 144
  Secretary-Generalship 40, 46,
    123
  staffing 21, 159–60n35
  supposed threat of 44, 68
  threats to 23, 100, 124, 130
UN General Assembly 39, 138
UN Human Rights Council 125
UN Peacekeeping Council 125
UN Security Council 39, 138, 141
  formation 123

  membership 6, 29, 123, 129,
    137, 172–3n7
  reform 124, 125, 127, 136, 137,
    138
  resolutions 29, 123, 138, 141,
    173n17
  veto system 139
UNHCR (United Nations High
  Commission for Refugees)
  97, 174n26
UNICEF (United Nations
  Children's Fund) 55
United Arab Republic 145
United Hashemite Kingdom 146
United Kingdom see Britain
United Nations see UN
United States:
  anti-immigration views 83
  Articles of Confederation 76
  Constitution 76, 105, 124, 136
  cultural appropriation, notions
    of 36–7
  Declaration of Independence 76
  defence spending and military
    capability 61, 62, 63, 131,
    136
  democracy, views on 94
  education 44, 168n17
  elections 19, 165n2
  environmental lobby 135
  film and television industry
    45–6, 162n21
  foreign aid 53, 120, 155n6,
    163n10
  foundation and development of
    union 75–6, 105
  freedom of speech 49, 53
  global citizenship, views on 22
  global governance, views on
    126, 127, 128, 129, 130–31

hegemony, erosion of 61, 116, 136, 146
immigrant population 84, 87, 88–9, 91
Iraq invasion (2003) 13, 60, 129, 131, 148
low-skilled population 27–8
NAFTA membership 71
national identity 39, 49, 53, 75, 76
Native Americans 75, 76, 91
pledge of allegiance 76, 166n12
race relations 25, 36, 75, 89
right to bear arms 49
social media usage 19, 159n28
states' rights 75, 76
tax avoidance 107, 110, 115–16
taxation 104, 105, 106, 108, 109, 110, 112–13, 114, 115–16, 118
and United Nations 122–4
visa system 30
voting systems 139
war on terror 62–3
see also Florida; Texas; Trump, Donald
universities see academia
Uyghur people 147, 164n21

Valmy, Battle of (1792) 11
Van Gogh, Vincent 37
Varoufakis, Yanis 4
Virginia School of political economy 105, 169n14

Wang Hui, China from Empire to Nation State 146
warfare see conflict, international
Wars of the Roses 174n30

wealth tax 57, 101–2, 110–11, 117–21, 138, 171n31, 172n51
Weber, Max 126–7
'West'/'Western', use of terms 6, 27, 31, 32–5, 161n6
Westphalia, Peace of (1648) 67, 165n1
Wilhelm I, German Kaiser 46
Willkie, Wendell, One World 9, 122–3
Wilson, Woodrow 77
World Bank 68, 71
World Cup (FIFA) 19, 163n5
'world history', studies of 43
World Trade Organization (WTO) 68, 123–4, 129
World's Largest Lesson (educational initiative) 55
Wriston, Walter, The Twilight of Sovereignty 67–8
WTO see World Trade Organization

Xi Jinping 113
Xinjiang 146, 147

Yassin, Nuseir, video blog 44–5
Yemen 52, 61, 73, 144, 145
YouTube (video-sharing website) 18–19, 158n24–5
Yugoslavia 10

Zakaria, Fareed 102
Zucman, Gabriel, The Hidden Wealth of Nations 106, 107, 113, 116, 170n19, 172n51